T0390276

CAMILLE BINET-DEZERT
PHOTOGRAPHY BY LINDA LOUIS
TRANSLATED BY GRACE McQUILLAN

Plant Dyes
MAKE YOUR OWN NATURAL FABRIC AND YARN DYES

Skyhorse Publishing

Contents

Preface

I was initially drawn to plant dyeing for the same reasons I recycle: I find real joy in creating something using only what I have on hand. To me, working within this constraint is incredibly inspiring. Now that I dye my own fabrics, I can easily produce the materials I need for my projects. One old bed sheet from a thrift store and I suddenly have unlimited color and pattern possibilities at my fingertips.

A few years ago, one of my embroidery instructors told me about a friend of hers whom she hadn't seen in several years. He'd apparently gotten "caught up in plant dyes." She didn't say anything else about it, but that one sentence has remained engraved in my memory. Only now do I fully understand what she meant. Be careful, dear reader, because the world you are about to discover is vast and marvelously addictive. . . .

There are many reasons plant dyeing is so enjoyable. It allows you to create your own unique fabrics and yarn, it's inexpensive, and the rich colors it will give you simply can't be compared with color from a chemical dye. But the real secret is this: What keeps people coming back to plant dyes again and again is the infinite number of surprises and variations that each one offers. This element of risk—in part due to chance, in part due to nature—is, quite honestly, a source of boundless pleasure. Dip two different pieces of cotton in the same dyebath and you will find two different shades when you pull them out. Unroll an eco-print and you'll rediscover the childlike joy of tearing open a goody bag. Arrange your frozen cubes of madder root and indigo dye on a piece of silk and savor the excitement of waiting to see what will happen.

I am not a chemist, nor am I a botanist. I learned how to use plant dyes largely on my own, with the help of a number of different books and websites, and I was able to put into practice what I had been studying thanks to a few workshops with botanist and dyer Élisabeth Dumont. I decided to write this book for anyone who's looking for an easy, simple way to get going on their first dye projects—just like I was a few years ago. I wanted to unite traditional techniques with newer, more experimental techniques. One section of this book is also dedicated exclusively to adding patterns and printing to your fabric because I have never found a book on dyeing that really takes the time to explain these things in depth.

I am committed to upcycling what would otherwise end up in a garbage can, and my creative decisions are guided by my concerns about waste. This book was written with that in mind. Unlike more conventional books on plant dyes, which tend to concentrate on traditional dye yielding plants, I have chosen to focus on plants that are common and readily available in urban areas: kitchen waste, tree bark, wilted bouquets, and edible plants you can buy in a store. That being said, I wanted to include a few traditional dye plants like indigo, oak gall, and madder root because of how remarkable their colors are and because I know you will enjoy working with them so much.

At the end of this book, you'll find ideas for at-home dye projects to work on all year long. These are quick and easy pieces that won't always require mordanting and will, I hope, inspire you to follow your own creative intuition for other projects.

Camille

Before
GETTING STARTED

The Dyer's Lexicon

Dyebath acidity or alkalinity: This is the pH of the bath. An acidic dyebath will have a pH between 1 and 7. An alkaline bath will have a pH between 7 and 14.

Finishing: A chemical treatment used to give textiles certain desirable properties. This can make it difficult for dye to bind to the fiber.

Cellulose fibers: These are fibers made from plants (cotton, flax, hemp . . .).

Protein fibers: These fibers come from animals (silk, wool, angora . . .).

Mordanting: This process prepares the fabric or yarn to help it absorb an intense, long-lasting plant color. The fibers are typically heated with a mordant (alum, soy, tannins . . .).

Modifying: This process alters the color of the fiber through the use of a second bath containing water and another substance (ferrous sulfate [iron], wood ash, etc.) that will react with the dye.

Tannins: Organic substances in the polyphenol family that are present in certain "tannic" plants. They react strongly to contact with metal salts.

EQUIPMENT

You can work with plant dyes in your kitchen, but make sure you use the right equipment and avoid using your personal cooking utensils whenever possible.

Cooking Pots

These pots should only be used for dyeing. Choose pots that can fit large pieces of fabric and that will allow your items to move freely in the pot. This will ensure even color.

If you are dyeing with tannic plants and using cast iron, this will affect your final result. The color will be absorbed more intensely and will appear somewhat darker.

Whenever possible, stick to stainless steel pots. You can use enameled cast iron pots, but make sure the enamel is not damaged because if your fabric does come into contact with the cast iron, the chemical reaction with plant tannins could cause staining.

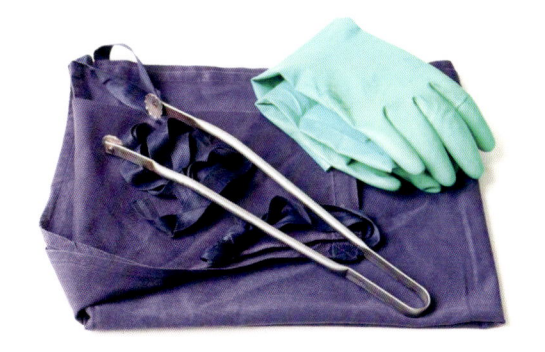

Protecting Yourself

Wear a large apron and gloves when handling certain plants that could stain your hands. A large pair of stainless-steel tongs will prove very useful for stirring your items and pulling them out of hot baths. Unlike wooden tongs, they are also easy to clean.

Tools

- Digital scale
- Immersion blender
- Small coffee grinder for grinding bark and roots
- Strainers and sieves
- Glass bottles/jars for storing dyebaths
- Corks, funnels, bottle brush
- pH strips can be helpful when working with certain plant dyes or modifiers. You can find them in the aquarium section at most garden stores.

Shibori

It won't be long before you fall in love with this folding and binding dye technique. For these projects, you will need a few extra supplies.

- Clothespins
- Small wooden blocks
- Rubber bands
- White twine
- Clamps
- Wooden rods

CHOOSING WHAT TO DYE

There are three major textile families and only two of them can be dyed. It is important to be able to distinguish between them.

SYNTHETIC TEXTILES

Synthetic textiles cannot be dyed naturally so let's rule them out now. Many people are unfortunately unaware of their impact on our environment and our health. These fabrics are made up of textile fibers derived from hydrocarbons. Manufacturing these fibers involves significant energy costs as well as high levels of toxic chemicals in the dye process. These fibers are not biodegradable and when synthetic textiles are washed, they release hydrocarbon microparticles which are not filtered by water purification plants and end up in our oceans as a result. Polyester, polyamide, acrylic, and elastane are the most widely used.

ARTIFICIAL TEXTILES

Artificial textiles are not the same as synthetic textiles, but they cannot be qualified as natural textiles, either. The fibers have undergone chemical treatment, but they are made using natural raw materials like cotton waste and wood. These are fabrics like rayon (also called viscose), acetate, and triacetate. These textiles can be dyed naturally.

NATURAL FIBERS

The natural fibers we are interested in for the purposes of this book can be divided into two categories.

Animal fibers: protein fibers

Thanks to the proteins in their makeup, fibers like wool and silk will absorb color easily with fantastic results. They also require a particular kind of mordanting.

Plant fibers: cellulose fibers

Plant fibers like cotton, flax, hemp, bamboo, ramie, and jute do not fix color as well as animal fibers and the results may not be as satisfying. Nevertheless, with a decent mordanting it is possible to achieve relatively intense and long-lasting colors. Organic fabrics that are unfinished and untreated will fix color better than other fabrics made with natural fibers.

WHAT SHOULD I PUT IN MY DYE POT?

You can dye pieces of fabric, light-colored clothing, and knitted or crocheted pieces like tablecloths or antique doilies. You can also put in hanks of wool yarn, embroidery thread, or macramé cords to create your own plant color palette for craft projects.

CAN I DYE A GARMENT MADE FROM SYNTHETIC AND CELLULOSE FIBERS (80% COTTON, 20% ELASTANE)?

Yes, but the dyed fabric will have flecks in it. Depending on the piece of clothing, this may or may not produce an attractive result.

CAN I DYE A STAINED GARMENT?

Dye will not cover up the stain—you will still see it. The only solution is to try to disguise the stain with other dye stains (see June, page 142) or shibori prints (page 108).

> To find out if a fiber is natural or synthetic, try burning a few threads. If a piece of crumbly ash forms, the fiber is natural. If the threads form a black cluster that looks like burned plastic, the fiber is synthetic.

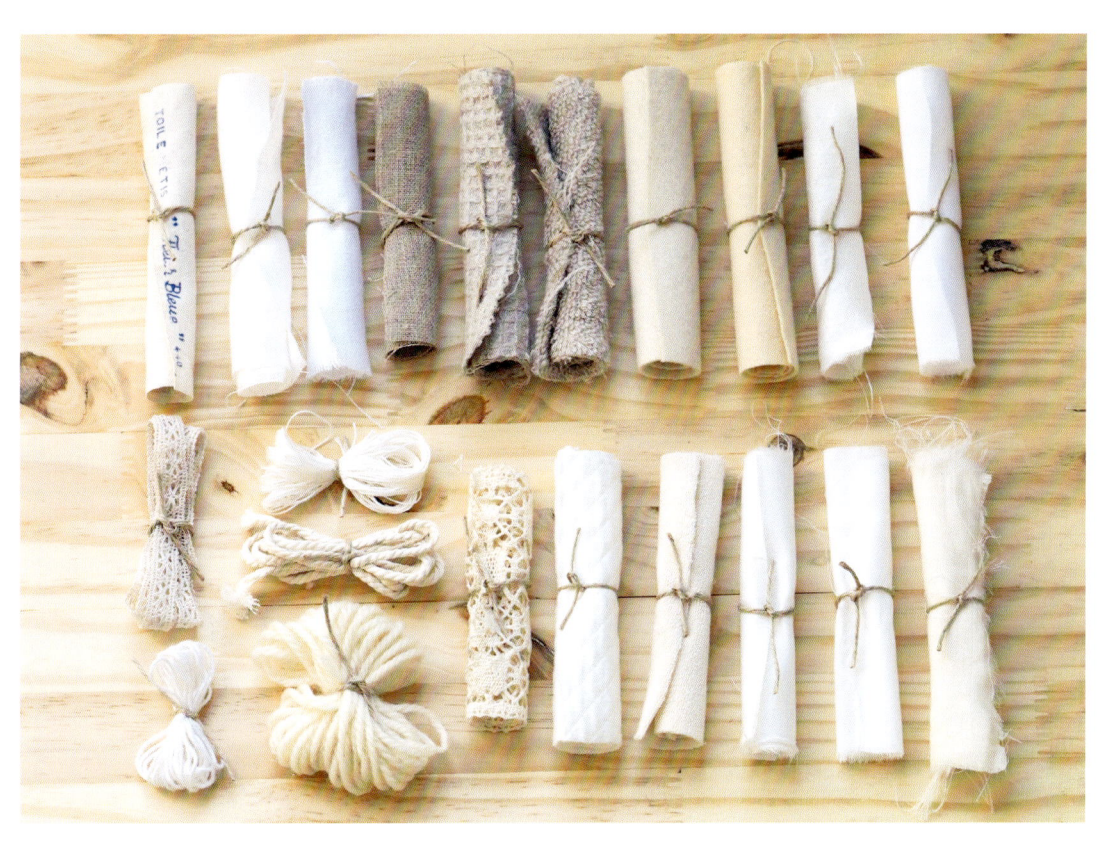

These are samples of the natural organic materials I used to make all of the projects in this book. From top to bottom and right to left: silk crepe, wild silk, unbleached woolen fabric, white wool, linen terry cloth, linen honeycomb towel, linen muslin, washed linen, métis linen (linen and cotton blend), cotton diaper, cotton voile, gabardine, cotton terry cloth, cotton matelasse, antique lace, samples of wool, rope, pearl cotton, stranded cotton, lace ribbon.

MORDANTING

The fibers you want to dye need to be treated with something that will allow the color to adhere to the fiber. Most of the time, this involves soaking and heating the fibers in water containing a mordant. Mordanting is the most complicated step in the dye process and good mordanting is the sign of an experienced dyer.

There are many ways to do this, and some techniques are more complicated than others. In this book, which is intended for beginners, we will only explore two methods in detail because they are easy and will give you good results for non-professional use. For those interested in learning about other mordanting techniques (aluminum acetate, cider vinegar, iron, tannins, or oil) and more environmentally friendly mordanting, I would invite you to consult the bibliography at the end of this book.

It should be noted that mordanting is not always necessary. If you are dyeing with heavily tannic plant-based dyes—known as substantive dyes—the fibers will absorb the dye without a mordant. This is the case for avocado, pomegranate, oak tree bark, walnut tree bark, oak gall, etc. Mordanting will, however, strengthen the color and durability of these dyes.

Mordanting with Alum

"Color-loving" substances are those that form a bridge between fibers and dyes. Metallic salts happen to be the best at it. Alum is used most frequently and is available in its natural or synthetic form. It is often used in the company of a second ingredient: cream of tartar. This is a powder made from crystals that form as a result of fermentation on the walls of wine barrels. Cream of tartar brightens and evens colors and augments alum's fixing power.

MORDANTING WITH ALUM AND CREAM OF TARTAR

Wool (fabric or ball of yarn)
1. Weigh the dry fibers and write down the weight. Wash the fibers and leave them to soak overnight in hot water (around 120°F [50°C]) with potassium carbonate (0.67 ounces/gallon [5 grams/liter]) or soap. Rinse.

2. Fill a stainless-steel pot with water and add the alum (10% of the weight of yesterday's dry fibers) and cream of tartar (optional, 6% weight-of-fiber [WOF]. Stir to dissolve the powders.

3. Place your pot over the heat and add your presoaked fibers.

4. Heat for one hour at a low boil. Turn off the heat and wait for the water to cool before removing the fibers. Wring them out and dry away from sunlight before dyeing.

Note:

Wool can be boiled without turning to felt as long as it is not subjected to thermal shock. This is why it is so important to let it cool down slowly in the mordant bath.

Silk
Silk can be mordanted at room temperature without being heated.

1. Fill a container with water and add your alum (30% WOF) and cream of tartar (optional, 15% WOF).

2. Once the powders have dissolved, add the presoaked silk to the container and let soak overnight. Rinse and dry away from sunlight or immediately proceed with your dyebath.

Cellulose fibers
Use the wool mordanting technique described above. You do not need to worry about felting with plant fibers, but you may wish to add more alum (20% WOF) to intensify the color. Most of the time, though, 10% WOF is enough.

Tip
You can reuse the liquid from your last mordanting session by adding fresh powder. This will save water and you won't have to dispose of large amounts of water containing metallic salts in your yard or down the drain.

Mordanting with Soy Milk

Soy milk, like animal milks (and urine!), has long been used to prepare fibers before mordanting. These milks all provide plant fibers with the proteins they are lacking—the very proteins that make animal fibers so perfect for dyeing—but soy milk can also be used as a mordant on animal fibers to reinforce the proteins that are already present.

Though it is not as strong or long-lasting a mordant as alum, it will still give you a satisfying result. Mordanting with soy milk is also easier and does not involve heat. Soy milk can be reused many times and, unlike alum, does not contain aluminum.

MORDANTING WITH SOY MILK FROM A CARTON

1. Purchase your soy milk (choose one without sugar or added ingredients; organic and local is best).

2. Depending on the amount of fibers you want to mordant, pour one or two quarts (one or two liters) of milk into a bowl.

3. After your fibers have been soaked in water and wrung out, add them to the bowl of milk.

4. Let soak for one or two days in a cool place to keep your milk from fermenting. If it does ferment, rinse or even wash the fibers if necessary to remove the unpleasant odor.

MORDANTING WITH SOYBEANS

For an even more effective result that is cheaper and more environmentally friendly, make your own soy milk.

STEP 1:

Soak 10.58 oz (300 grams) of soybeans in a large quantity of water for one day. They should double in size.

STEP 2:

When the soybeans have taken on a more elongated shape, rinse them and throw away the soaking water.

STEP 3:

Transfer your soybeans and a small amount of water to a tall container (like a jar) and blend.

STEP 4:

Stop blending when you reach a pulpy consistency.

STEP 5:
Mix your pulp with three quarts (three liters) of water and let sit overnight.

STEP 6:
The next day, strain your milk and press any residue through a strip of gauze or cheesecloth to extract as much liquid as possible.

STEP 7:
You can compost the leftover residue, but don't eat it. This is not a recipe for drinkable soy milk.

STEP 8:
The milk is now ready to mordant fibers.

I prefer not adding water to my milk, so I use the same milk several times until it ferments.

A Little Experiment

I mordanted these five old table napkins five different ways before dyeing them in the same madder dyebath. Then, I machine-washed them at 104°F (40°C) ten times to see how well the color held. In the photographs on the next two pages, you'll see a clear difference in how each mordant affected its napkin's color after washing and exposure to sunlight.

From left to right on the first photo and from top to bottom on the second photo:
1- No mordant 2- No mordant. Soaked in white vinegar, which is said to prevent color transfer.
3- Mordanted with soy milk 4- Mordanted with 10% alum and 6% cream of tartar 5- Mordanted with 20% alum only.

How Can I Make My Colors Last Longer?

How long your color lasts will depend on several factors:

- Thorough mordanting should make your fabrics colorfast and help the dye stand up to wear and tear.

- Your choice of fiber (animal fiber will hold onto color better because it will have absorbed it better).

- The length of time your fibers spend in the dyebath (the longer they are in the bath, the longer the color will last).

- The dye type. Some dyes (weld, indigo, madder, dahlia, avocado) are classified as "grand-teint" because they resist fading better than "petit-teint" dyes.

- Exposure to light: avoid exposing your fabric too often to sunlight (both when drying and if you decide to display a piece near a window).

- Whenever you wash your fibers, use natural detergent that does not contain chemical bleaching agents. I sometimes add a little Marseille soap to my detergent. This combination intensifies the color of certain dyes because Marseille soap is alkaline and behaves like wood ash. Alternately, use 1.7 ounces (50 milliliters) liquid Castile soap with 1 quart (about 1 liter) water and 2 tablespoons baking soda.

DYEING METHODS

Here are two ways to dye your fibers. The first is the most common method and the dyebath is prepared just about identically for 90% of plants. The second method requires a little less energy. Other techniques like vat dyeing with indigo will be explained on page 95.

Hot Dyeing

This method is explained in detail here. Later in the book, return to this page whenever you need to.

ONION SKINS

STEP 1:
Weigh out a fair amount of onion skins (or whatever plant material you are using). Tear or cut into small pieces. The smaller the pieces are, the more dye will be extracted.

STEP 2:
Submerge the skins in your pot of water. Try to use rainwater if you live somewhere with hard tap water because the high mineral content could alter your end result. You can also add a teaspoon of white vinegar to soften the water.

STEP 3:
Heat for one hour to extract the dye.

STEP 4:
Remove all of your plant material from the bath and press it through a piece of cloth or the bottom of a strainer to extract as much liquid as you can. Compost the rest.

STEP 5:
After mordanting your fabric (see page 16), soak it to open the fibers. Then add it to the dye pot and heat the bath.

STEP 6:
One hour at a low boil should be enough for a pleasing result. Remove the fibers sooner if you don't want the color to be too dark. Otherwise, just let them cool in the bath. You can even leave them submerged for several days.

STEP 7:
Submerge the dyed fibers in a basin of soapy water to rinse them. Wring them out over a sink and rinse again if needed until the water runs clear. Dry away from sunlight. The first time you wash your dyed fabrics, wash them separately so they don't stain your other laundry.

Solar Dyeing

This dyeing method may not require as much energy, but it does demand a certain amount of patience. In solar dyeing, plant material is added to a jar of water and the sealed jar is left alone so sunlight and time can do their work. After a few days, the plant dye will have permeated the water and you can squeeze the plant material to extract any remaining colorant. Then remove the plant material, seal your fibers in the jar with the water, and leave the jar in the sun for a few days. Shake the jar once in a while or open it to stir your fabric to make sure the dye can penetrate evenly.

These two methods allow you to dye whole pieces of fabric a more or less solid, even color. Other methods for adding a second or third color or a pattern (eco-print, ice dyeing, etc.) will be explained in the third section of the book (Patterns and Printing).

Tip
You may decide to combine these two methods for some of your projects. For instance, you could extract the dye over heat and then place the jarred dyebath in the sun for a few days with your fibers inside.

MODIFIERS

Using modifiers may seem unnecessary when you're just starting out, but before long you won't want to dye anything without them! Modifiers are used after the initial dyebath to change the color you have obtained naturally with the plant material. "Shifting" the color this way can be achieved by either modifying the dye's pH—its acidity or alkalinity—or creating a tannin reaction with iron. As you might imagine, modifiers significantly expand the palette of colors that each dye can produce. Modifiers should be used in a separate container, not the dyebath. This allows you to save the dyebath for a later project. After the initial dyebath, do not rinse the fabric before using modifiers. When preparing your modifier, you will need to dilute it in water. Throw in one cup per quart (liter) of water to start and then adjust as needed depending on how the initial color is affected.

Alkaline Modifiers

These have a pH higher than 7. Wood ash, slaked lime, and crushed chalk (Meudon whiting powder is one example) are the most frequently used. Slaked lime and crushed chalk can be found in specialty stores and wood ash water is easy to make. In addition to being a wonderful modifier, wood ash can also be used as a household cleaning product. Marseille soap is also very basic and can help modify certain dyes. Or see page 25 for a Castile soap detergent formula.

STEP 1:
Use a sieve to eliminate large chunks of charcoal and other metallic waste from your wood ash.

STEP 2:
When your ash is fine and clean, cover it with water. Add three volumes of water for every volume of ash.

STEP 3:
Shake and let the container sit for a day or two. Shake occasionally.

STEP 4:
When the water is viscous on the surface, like soapy water, the ash is ready.

STEP 5:
Strain the mixture through a cloth (not a sieve or a strainer) to make sure it is filtered as finely as possible. Use gloves because wood ash can be irritating to the skin, particularly on your hands.

Acidic Modifiers

These have a pH lower than 7. I use primarily white vinegar, apple cider vinegar, and lemon juice.

Iron Modifiers

These modifiers contain iron components that react with the tannins present in certain plant dyes. There are two kinds that are both easy to make at home. Use in limited quantities on wool and silk because iron will attack these fibers.

FERROUS SULFATE (IRON) BATH

Add a teaspoon of powdered ferrous sulfate to a quart (liter) of water. Once mixed, you can save this "iron water" for months. Powdered ferrous sulfate is an inexpensive green powder that can be purchased at garden centers. The powder is obtained through mineral oxidation and is used to get rid of moss on lawns. This bath can be used as soon as you make it and does not need time to activate.

IRON ACETATE OR "NAIL SOUP"

Fill a jar three-quarters of the way with water and the remaining quarter with vinegar. Add old iron nails or iron filings. You will have to wait one week for the solution to activate before you can use it.

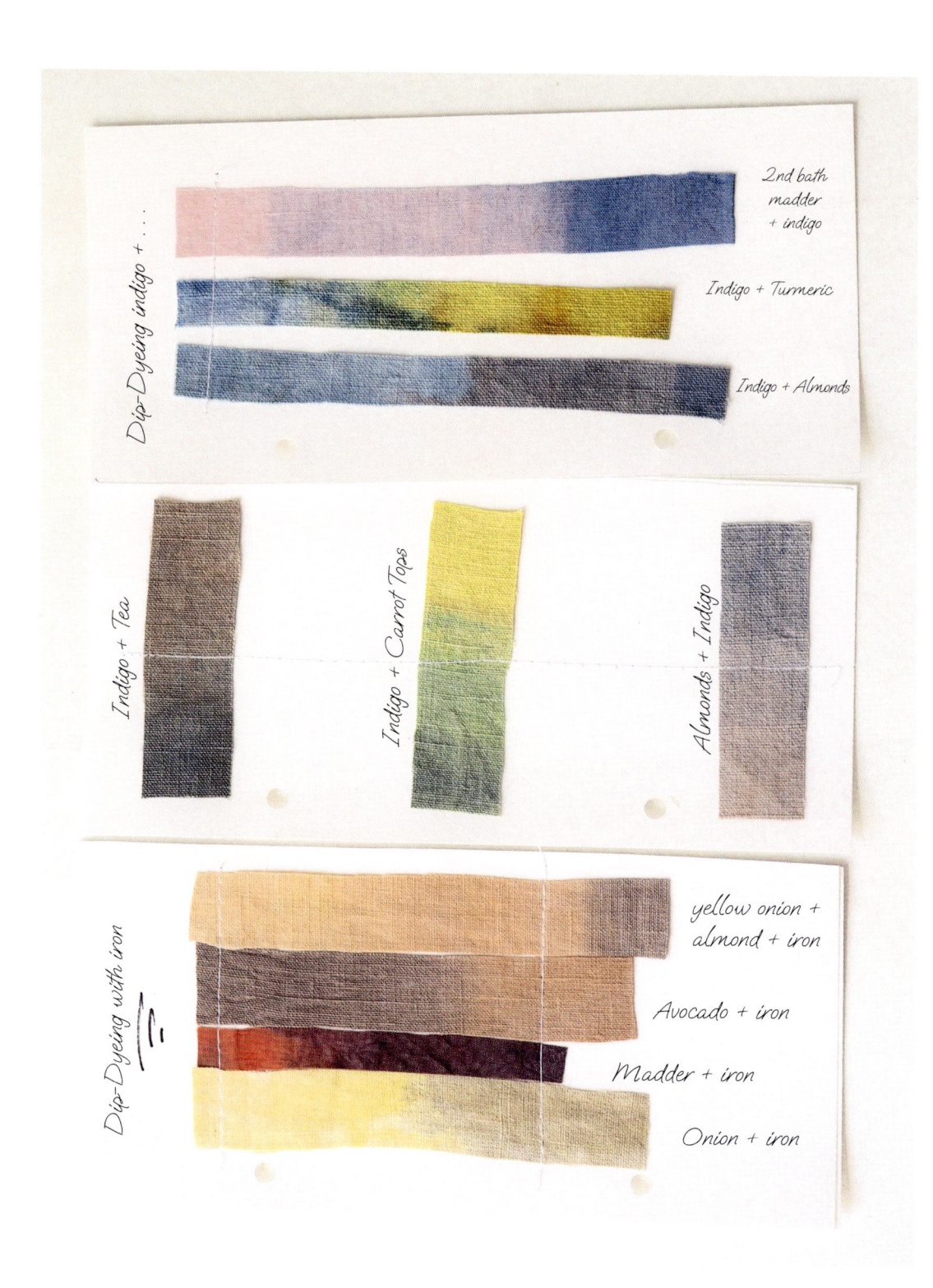

Dip-Dyeing indigo + ...

2nd bath madder + indigo

Indigo + Turmeric

Indigo + Almonds

Indigo + Tea

Indigo + Carrot Tops

Almonds + Indigo

Dip-Dyeing with iron

yellow onion + almond + iron

Avocado + iron

Madder + iron

Onion + iron

KEEPING A DYE JOURNAL

This is one task that is going to seem tedious, but it is essential if you want to keep track of your dye experiments and replicate colors easily later on. As you begin testing more and more different fabrics and dyes, take the time to toss swatches of your fabrics into containers of your prepared modifiers to create a visual record of the variations that are possible with the plants you have used. Then start organizing everything in a notebook or binder, which is what I use. I think binders are easier to handle and I like being able to pull out a page if necessary to see how two colors look side by side.

DYE JOURNAL TIPS

1. Attach your swatches to each page with masking tape or staple them. I sew them on, but it does take longer.

2. Make a note of the kind of fiber you used (animal, plant, etc.).

3. As soon as the dyeing process is complete (this is not required but does give the best results), submerge your swatches in two or three different modifiers. Try to give priority to modifiers that cover a wide pH range to give yourself a variety of shades and tones to record in your journal.

4. Be careful not to mix up the swatches while they are drying.

5. Make a note of how long each dyebath took, where and when you found your plants, the best dye combinations, etc.

Tip
To save time, I made my own stamps by cutting out letters from old stamps I bought secondhand.

The Dyer's 10 Golden Rules

1. Prioritize dyeing wool, silk, or antique/organic plant-based fibers.

2. Use stainless-steel pots if possible.

3. Thorough mordanting will augment color absorption and resistance to fading but is optional when using tannic plants. As a general rule, do not dry your items in direct sunlight.

4. Mordant fabrics before dyeing and mordant several at one time.

5. Gather plant material all year long and dry for storage.

6. Always use plant material that has been shredded or finely blended in order to maximize its dyeing potential.

7. The longer you heat the fabric in the dyebath, the more intense and long-lasting the color will be.

8. Reuse your dyebaths several times by storing them in glass bottles/jars.

9. Always keep a few modifiers on hand to add variety to your fabric colors.

10. Clean your hands with lemon juice to remove black traces of tannin from under your nails and clean any dye from your sink with hot water, sodium percarbonate, and lemon.

Natural
DYES

Yellows and Tans

In this book I have singled out plants that are either common kitchen ingredients or food waste. This is why in this section I will only be discussing onions, turmeric, and pomegranate. You should know, though, that there are many plants that make yellow dye—in fact, they are the most commonly found dye plants in nature! Weld, for instance, is a grand-teint dye that turns fibers a clear, brilliant yellow and can be grown in your own backyard. The same is true for dahlias (harvest them when the flowers start to wilt), goldenrod, dyer's broom, Queen Anne's Lace, meadowsweet, linden blossoms, dandelions, and more.

WOOL **SILK** **LINEN** **COTTON**

IRON

ACETATE **WOOD ASH**

Time: 20 minutes.

YELLOW ONION SKINS

Working with onion skins is enjoyable and easy, especially when you're just starting out. Onions are inexpensive and their dye always yields a strong color. Even though mordanting will make the color more intense and long-lasting, it is not a requirement in this case.

Collect your onion skins in a brown paper bag in your kitchen. For a step-by-step guide to dyeing with onion skins, see page 26. Don't hesitate to pull your fabric out of the bath fairly quickly (after about twenty minutes) if you want a bright yellow. Any longer and the color will begin to appear dark and dull.

RED ONION SKINS

I never mix red and yellow onion skins because the two have their own unique dye colors. Red onions offer a green-brown, bronze color that I find quite interesting.

Using iron modifiers (particularly on cellulose fibers) changes the yellow dye color to olive green.

TURMERIC

Turmeric is another dye that is easy to use. If you buy it at the store in powdered form, you don't even have to extract the dye yourself.

DYEBATH PREPARATION

1. Over heat, measure and add 5 teaspoons (15 grams) of ground turmeric to three quarts (about three liters) of water (this is a guideline—feel free to adjust).

2. Add your fibers directly to the pot (with or without mordanting ahead of time).

3. Heat for around one hour.

Your fibers will emerge from the bath a vibrant yellow, but unfortunately this color will deepen and oxidize over time.

To prevent this, never dry a dyed garment in direct sunlight.

You do not have to mordant your fabric before dyeing with turmeric, but it will help preserve the dye color.

Modifiers will have very little effect on fibers dyed with turmeric.

POMEGRANATE

This is one of my favorite dyes—it's long-lasting and turns a wonderful deep gray color after being modified with iron water.

DYEBATH PREPARATION

1. Cut the fruit into quarters and remove the seeds to use in a dessert.

2. Now chop the skin into small pieces. You can also dry the skins and save them for later use.

3. Follow the instructions for hot dyeing. Whenever I work with pomegranate, I like to use an immersion blender halfway through to extract as much dye as possible.

Pomegranates are high in tannin, so mordanting is not necessary (even though it will give you a better result). Like the onion skin dyebaths we saw earlier, this is a dye that allows you to repurpose food waste. It reacts strongly with iron and is one of the best dyes for painting with iron water and stamping (see Creating Designs with Iron Water, page 105).

Greens

Nature offers us this beautiful paradox: When we look at our natural surroundings, green is abundant, but once we start trying to adhere it to a piece of fiber, this same color becomes very difficult to obtain. There are some yellow plant dyes that will give you a color that verges on green, but the most reliable way to achieve true green color is to modify with iron water or combine yellow and blue dyebaths. On the following pages you'll find out which plants are best at yielding that sought-after green (with a little help from modifiers). As you will see, this process works best on wool.

CARROT TOPS

Carrot tops so often end up as food waste, but they deserve to be put to use instead! Buy one bunch of carrots with the tops still on, then remove the greens and hang them upside down to dry in a dark, well-ventilated part of your home. Alternatively, you can use fresh carrot tops.

DYEBATH PREPARATION

1. You will need the greens from one bunch of carrots to dye around 3.5 ounces (100 grams) of fibers. If you're looking for a deep color and are using cellulose fibers, you will need at least two bunches of carrots.

2. Follow the instructions for hot dyeing (page 26).

Without modifiers, this dye will give you a very pale yellow green on cellulose fibers and a bright yellow color on wool. Iron baths will shift the color to gray green.

WOOL

SILK LINEN COTTON

IRON

WOOD ASH

ACETATE

THYME

Depending on what material you are dyeing, thyme (like tarragon, rosemary, and sage) yields a yellow dye or a pale yellow that is almost green. Using an iron bath on the fibers will change the color to pale green.

DYEBATH PREPARATION

Chop up sprigs of thyme into small pieces. You will need quite a bit if you want the color to be noticeable on cellulose* fibers, so harvesting wild thyme is probably the best option. Submerge your sprigs in three quarts (about three liters) of water.

WOOL   **SILK**   **LINEN**   **COTTON**

IRON

ACETATE   **WOOD ASH**

ARTICHOKE

I will say it again: your discarded cooking ingredients deserve a second chance before heading for the garbage can! After you eat the artichoke hearts and leaves, set aside the rest. You can also use the leaves of the artichoke plant if you have any in your vegetable garden.

- -

DYEBATH PREPARATION

1. Chop up the stem and small leaves from two or three artichokes to dye 5.3 ounces (150 grams) of fiber. Compost the fluffy parts of the artichoke heart—we won't be using those. And of course, keep the heart to eat.

2. Follow the instructions for hot dyeing (page 26). Halfway through, break up the artichoke pieces with an immersion blender to help extract the dye.

- -

Using wood ash on silk will give you a superbly luminous yellow.

Beiges, Browns, and Blacks

Beige and brown can be extracted easily from some plants, but grays and blacks (like most of the greens) must be created artificially with an iron bath.

WOOL SILK LINEN COTTON

IRON

ACETATE

WOOD ASH

BRAMBLE LEAVES

This is a straightforward and inexpensive dye to work with because bramble leaves are easy to find in nature and you shouldn't have trouble gathering large quantities for your projects. Remember to bring gloves and shears whenever you are harvesting.

Bramble branches can also be used for dyeing. Dry them out to use later.

Without a modifier, you will obtain a pale beige color that you can deepen using wood ash. Iron water, on the other hand, will change the color to a lovely, brilliant gray. Wool fibers will take on an olive green color.

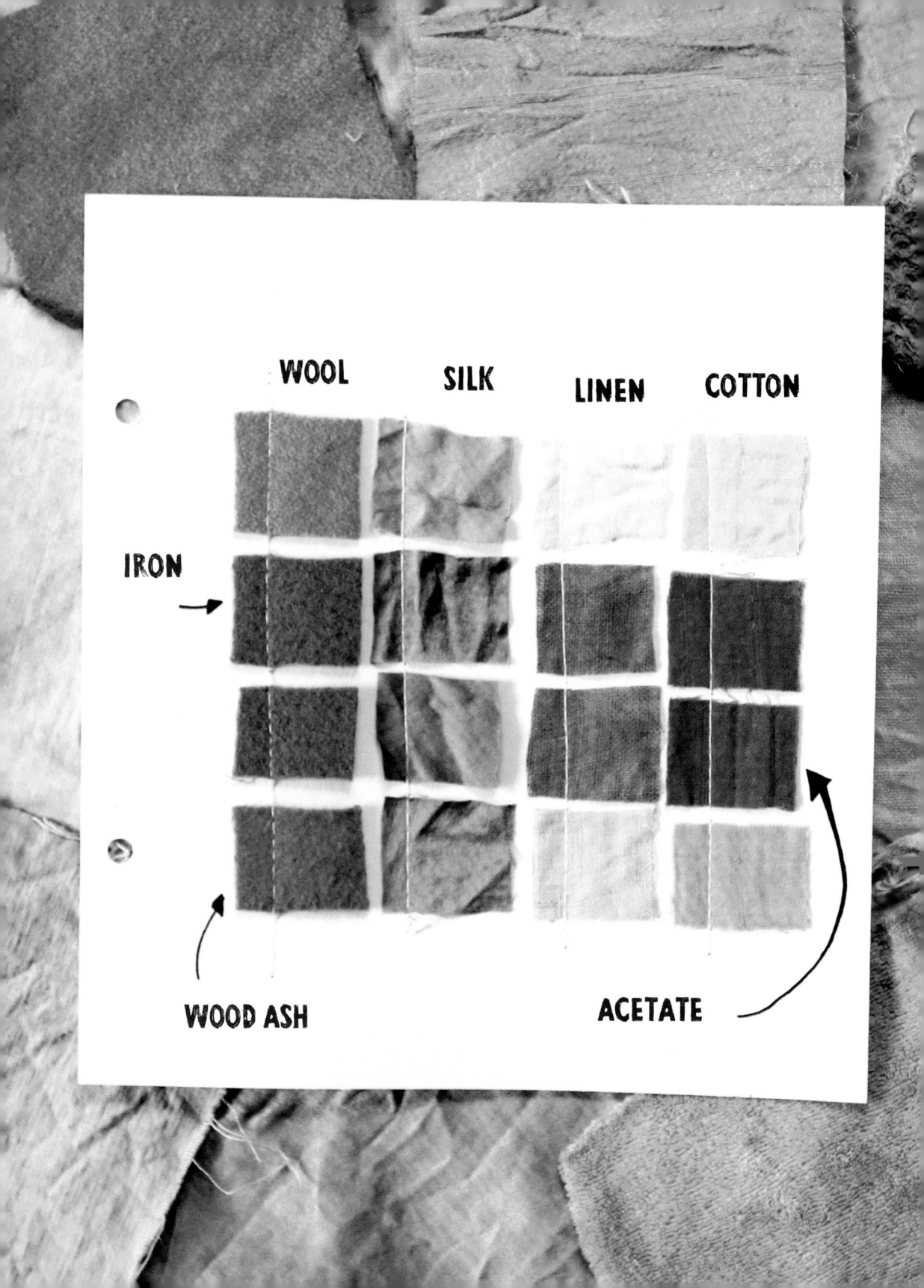

EUCALYPTUS

You'll love working with eucalyptus because every dye project fills your kitchen with its fresh perfume. Dyeing with eucalyptus is the perfect way to use up any leftover parts of a bouquet that has been sitting in your house for several days.

DYEBATH PREPARATION

1. Fill the dye pot with plant material—no need to hold back. You will need double the weight of fiber (200% WOF) in eucalyptus leaves if you want to get strong color on cellulose fibers.

2. Follow the instructions for hot dyeing (page 26).

There are several varieties of eucalyptus and you will get a slightly different shade with each one, but your fibers will always turn out beige and brown. You can shift the color to gray with an iron bath.

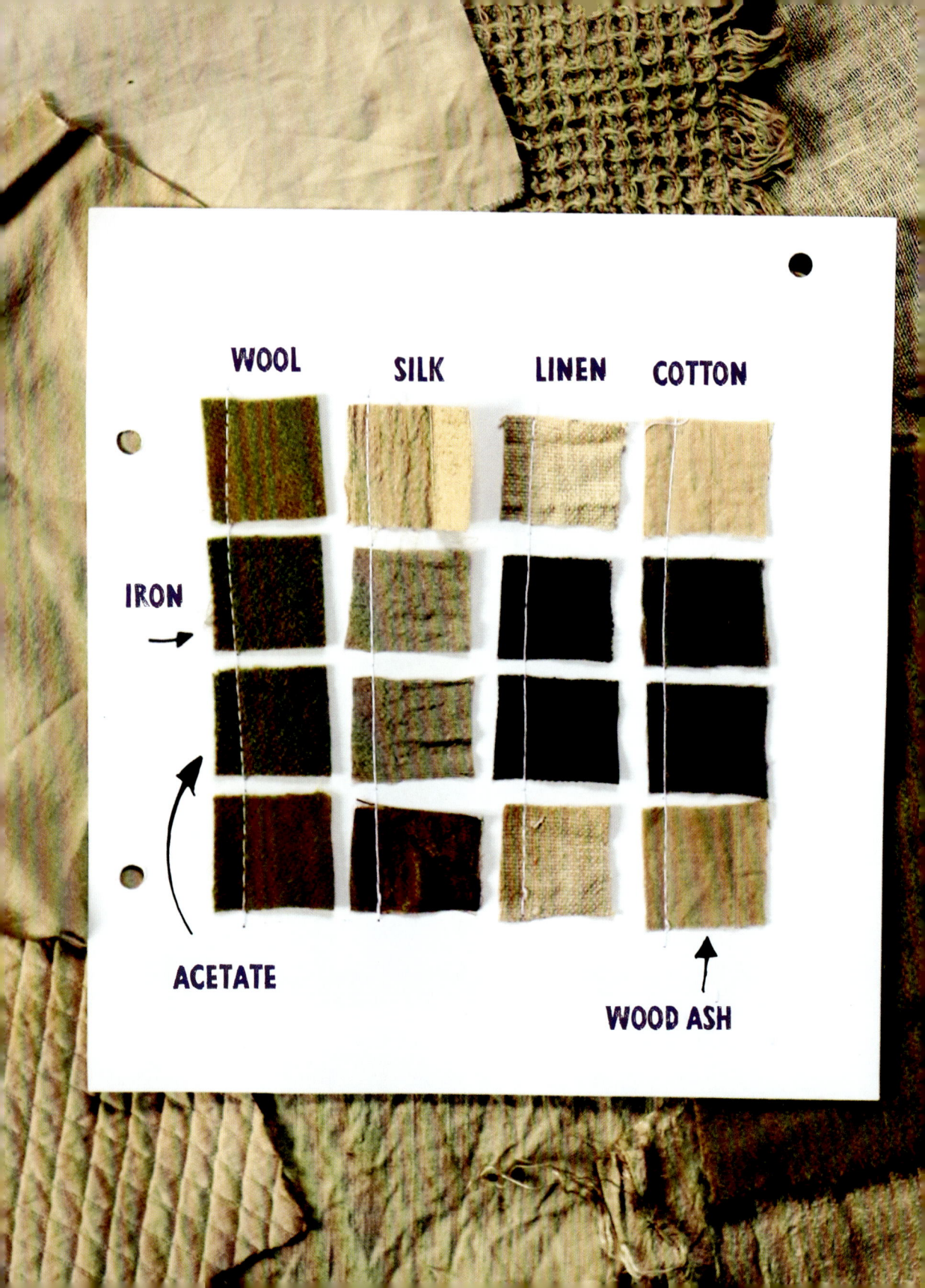

ACACIA

When acacia season arrives, buy yourself a big, beautiful bouquet (if you can) and wait until the flowers have wilted slightly before dyeing anything. Without a modifier, your fabrics will come out a pinky beige color, but an iron bath will change the color to gray.

DYEBATH PREPARATION

1. Use shears to cut up the stems, leaves, and flowers (the whole bouquet!).

2. Follow the instructions for hot dyeing (page 26).

Acacia is worth trying for the rich frosted chestnut color you can get on silk submerged in wood ash.

Dye can be extracted from larger branches, too. Dry them out and store for later use.

Without modifiers, you will get a pale beige that can be deepened using wood ash. Iron baths will give you bright gray or olive green if you are using wool.

WOOL   SILK   LINEN   COTTON

IRON

WOOD ASH

ACETATE

OAK TREE BARK

Oak trees are found all over North America, so this should be an easy project to tackle. To harvest the bark, you will need a hammer and a small chisel or screwdriver to break off a few pieces without damaging the inside of the tree.

DYEBATH PREPARATION

1. Grind up the bark using a small electric coffee grinder.

2. If you don't have a coffee grinder, remove the softened bark from the dyebath halfway through the process and cut it into smaller pieces. Then return the bark to the dyebath to finish extracting.

3. Follow the instructions for hot dyeing (page 26).

If you use an iron modifier, your fibers will take on a gray-black tone. Oak leaves and acorns can also be used for dyeing.

BLACK TEA

If you have old containers of black tea hiding in your cupboards, use them up with this kitchen-friendly dye!

Heat water in your dye pot with some strong black tea (30% WOF) and follow the instructions for hot dyeing (page 26).

You can achieve similar results with coffee grounds or boiled coffee.

WOOL SILK LINEN COTTON

IRON

WOOD ASH

ACETATE

WALNUT HULLS

For centuries, walnut has been one of the most widely used dyes in Europe. It is considered a grand-teint dye because of how well its color holds up to washing and exposure to light and you can achieve excellent results without mordanting ahead of time.

DYEBATH PREPARATION

1. Gather walnut hulls that are still green in the fall and let them ferment in a jar filled with water. They can be stored for several years before use. When you're ready to dye, strain out the husks and add the liquid to your dyebath. This method will yield the best results.

2. You can also dry the husks instead, which allows them to oxidize and turn black. Once dried, follow the instructions for hot dyeing (page 26).

Modifiers will have little effect on the natural color result.

You can also dye fibers brown with leaves and bark from the walnut tree.

Pinks and Reds

Pale pinks make frequent appearances in the plant dyer's pot thanks to the tannins in certain kinds of tree bark and a variety of food waste items. These pinks turn to gray in an iron bath. Alkaline baths, by contrast, will deepen and strengthen the natural pink color.

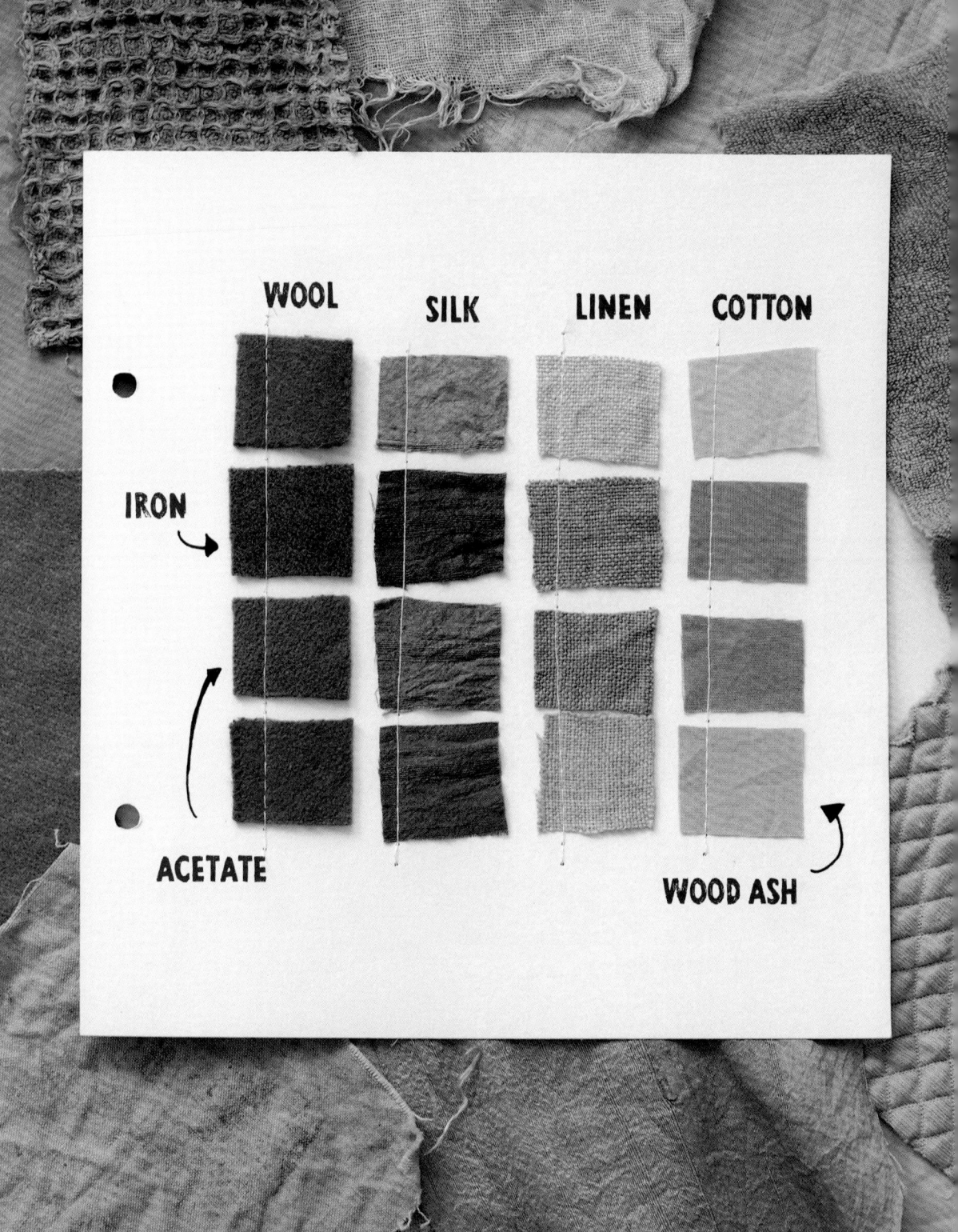

HEATHER

Heather is a common plant in many parts of Europe and North America and should be easy to find in garden centers if you do not have any growing wild in a forest near your home. To create the pinks seen here, use only the dried flowers from the plant.

DYEBATH PREPARATION

Make sure you have 50% WOF in dried heather flowers. Heather is also known for the beautiful yellow dye it produces. If that's what you're looking for, you'll have to use the woody stems of the plant, too.

BIRCH

Birch trees are found in many parts of North America and their bark makes a wonderfully effective plant dye. Bring a small hammer and chisel or screwdriver when you harvest the bark so you don't injure the tree more than you have to.

DYEBATH PREPARATION

1. Weigh out your birch bark (about 50% WOF, but you can also use less) and submerge in a pot of water. Bring to a boil.

2. Halfway through, when the bark has started to soften, remove the bark from the bath and cut it into smaller pieces. Return to the bath.

3. Alternatively, you can run the pieces of softened bark through a small coffee grinder.

4. Now, follow the instructions for hot dyeing (page 26).

Remember to gather bark that has already fallen to the ground before harvesting bark that is still on the tree.

WOOL SILK LINEN COTTON

IRON

ACETATE

WOOD ASH

ALMONDS

This dye is made with the fuzzy green outer covering of the unripe almond fruit. You can use fresh green almonds or harvest old hulls that have been forgotten on the tree.

The nuts that were used to dye these fabric swatches were harvested on the tree in December, months after the almond season in France had ended. Even though the hulls had already turned black, they still gave me the pink I was looking for.

DYEBATH PREPARATION

1. If using fresh green almonds, scrape off the green outer coverings and soak in water.

2. If the almonds are old, submerge the hulls in the dyebath first to soften them. Halfway through cooking, remove from the pot, let cool slightly, and then scrape off the outer covering with a knife.

3. Add the hulls to a separate bowl with a little bit of water from your dye pot. Use an immersion blender to blend the mixture into a pulp. Return this pulp to the dyebath.

4. Next, follow the instructions for hot dyeing (page 26).

AVOCADO

This is a fascinating and gorgeous grand-teint dye. Avocado skins and stones are something we so often throw away in our kitchens. This is a great way to use them.

DYEBATH PREPARATION

1. Every time you eat an avocado, scrape out any remaining flesh with a teaspoon and clean the skin thoroughly. Clean the stone and dry both in a well-ventilated area.

2. Tear four or five avocado skins into small pieces and submerge along with a few avocado stones (whole) in three quarts (approximately three liters) of water and boil for one hour.

3. Halfway through, use an immersion blender to break down your plant material in the dyebath to extract additional dye.

4. Follow the instructions for hot dyeing (page 26).

You will get a solid pale pink color that will increase in intensity with every wash, especially if you use natural detergent or Marseille soap (or see page 25 for a Castile soap detergent formula). If you use an iron bath, the pink will turn to an equally lovely purple gray.

Next time you eat out at a Japanese or Mexican restaurant, ask if you can have their avocado waste and store it in your freezer.

HIBISCUS

Hibiscus flowers are easy to find in organic stores on the tea aisle. If you've ever made your own bissap (hibiscus tea) before, you probably already know what a powerful colorant these flowers are!

DYEBATH PREPARATION

1. Weigh out your dried flowers (about 50% WOF).

2. Steep for one hour, strain out the flowers, and submerge your premordanted fibers.

3. Follow the instructions for hot dyeing (page 26).

Unfortunately, on cellulose fibers the result is not terribly exciting and, as a general rule, hibiscus is not the most resistant of dyes. If you are lucky enough to have a hibiscus plant in your yard, you can pick and dry the flowers yourself.

COCHINEAL

I am about to make one small exception here—cochineal is the name of an insect, not a plant. These small creatures can be found in Mexico, where they live on cacti. Dyers can purchase them in powdered form from specialty stores.

DYEBATH PREPARATION

1. Dissolve 0.14 ounces (4 grams) of powder in three quarts (approximately three liters) of water.

2. Add your premordanted (optional) and presoaked fibers to the dyebath. For these swatches I used 7.05 ounces (200 grams) of fibers.

3. Add 2 teaspoons of white vinegar to make your bath acidic and intensify the color.

4. Heat for around 45 minutes.

Cochineal is also a common food dye and is the only natural colorant that produces such a bright pink. This powder is highly concentrated, so you won't need very much to get a deep color even if you're using cellulose fibers. With 0.35 ounces (10 grams) you can dye anywhere from 1.1 pounds (500 grams) to 11 pounds (5 kilograms) of fibers, depending on the intensity of the color you're looking for.

WOOL SILK LINEN COTTON

ACETATE

WOOD ASH

IRON

MADDER

Madder is the red dye plant *par excellence* and has been used in France for centuries as a grand-teint dye. You can find it in specialty stores. It produces especially pleasing results on cellulose fibers.

DYEBATH PREPARATION

1. Weigh out your powder (30% WOF).

2. Add the powder to the dyebath water. Just this once, you will need to use hard water. Instead of rainwater, use tap water and feel free to add a tablespoon of lime or chalk. All of this will intensify the red color.

3. Make sure the temperature of your bath is no higher than 140°F (60°C) (check with a cooking thermometer). If it gets too hot, the red will darken and turn brown.

4. Mordant and soak your fibers (mordanting is required). Add them to the dyebath and heat for one hour. Rinse in soapy water and dry away from sunlight.

The root of the madder plant has to be ground into powder to be used as a dye. You can buy it already prepared.

Blues and Purples

Blue is rare in the world of plant dyeing, but once a dyer has managed to capture it, in my experience that individual is very excited to be able to add it to his or her repertoire. Indigo is a magical plant that will consistently give you deep, incredibly resistant color and does not require mordanting your fabrics beforehand. For a while, you'll find yourself wanting to throw everything you can get your hands on into the indigo vat. Luckily, there are plenty of kits available that make it easy to put together an iron indigo vat at home. You can toss it out in the yard when it is exhausted because it doesn't contain any toxic products. When you're not using indigo, you can dye fabrics blue with the water left over from soaking black beans. The color is not as deep and resistant as indigo, but it is a way to use water that would otherwise be thrown away. The beans are unaffected by this process and can be prepared normally.

WOOL   SILK   LINEN   COTTON

IRON

ACETATE

WOOD ASH

BLACK BEANS

Black beans are easy to find in most stores. Look for dried black beans, which can often be purchased at natural food stores, online, or even in regular grocery stores.

DYEBATH PREPARATION

1. Soak a pack of black beans in twice its volume of water. Wait 24 hours.

2. Strain and set aside the beans to cook later. Pour the black juice into your dye pot. Add a little water if needed.

3. Heat the pot with your premordanted fibers. The blue won't appear right away, and the mixture will appear purple-pink at first.

4. When the blue is fairly pronounced, remove the fibers and rinse them.

This blue color is not as resistant as indigo and will turn gray over time as it is exposed to light.

OAK GALL

When an insect makes a hole in a young oak branch to lay its eggs, the oak tree forms a small ball around the eggs. Once the larvae arrive at maturity, they escape through a tiny hole in the ball. These balls can be harvested at the end of summer and dried.

DYEBATH PREPARATION

1. Grind the nuts into powder with a small electric coffee grinder.

2. Weigh out your powder (use 30% WOF).

3. Follow the instructions for hot dyeing (page 26). If you want to create black right in the bath, add one teaspoon of ferrous sulfate powder directly to the dyebath. You could also follow this process with an iron bath.

Oak galls are prized in dyeing because they are so high in tannins. In fact, some dyers even use them as mordants.

When accompanied by ferrous sulfate in the dyebath or in a separate iron bath, oak gall will yield a beautiful black color that at times is almost purple. Fibers do not need to be mordanted before dyeing.

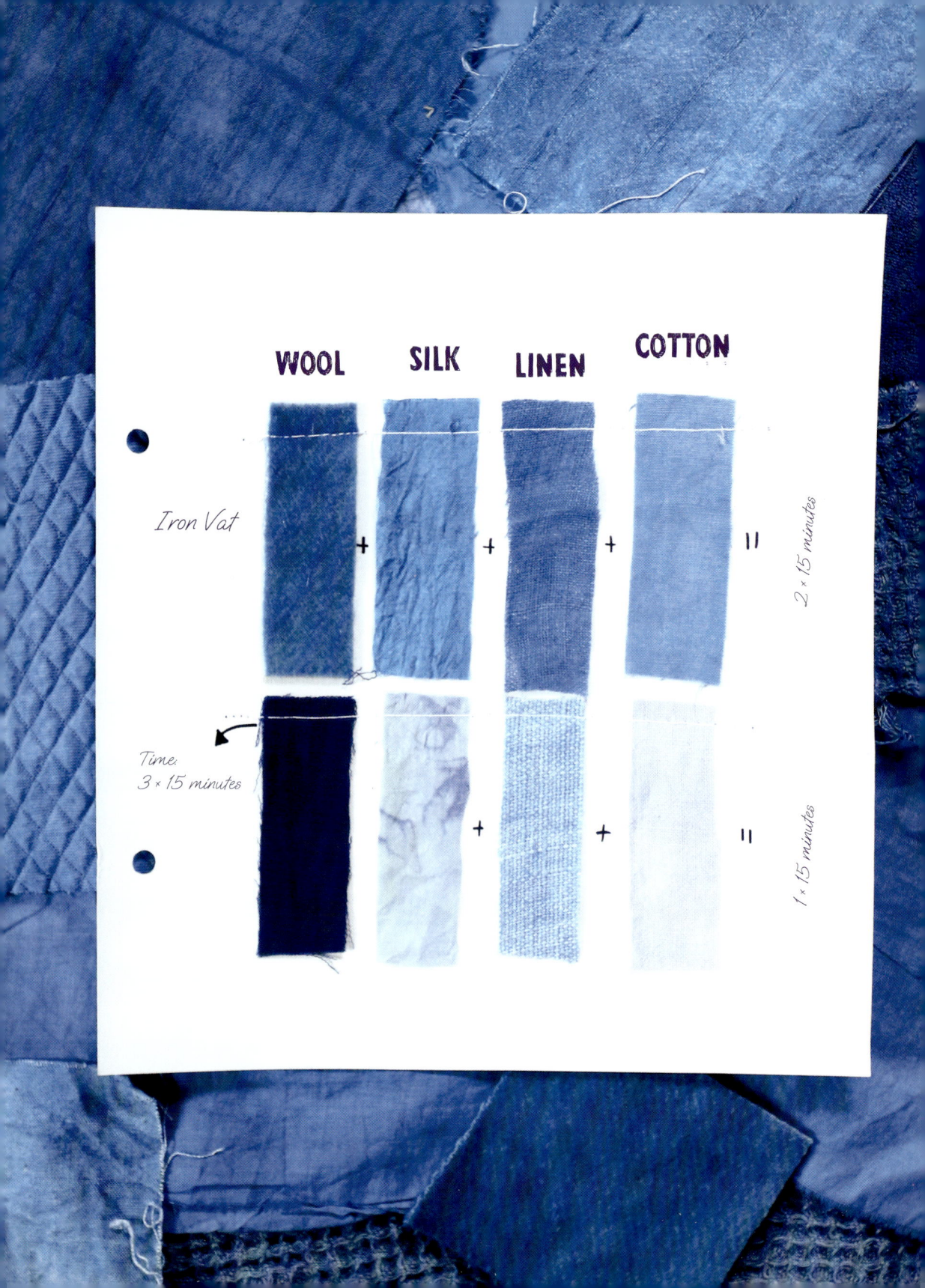

INDIGO

Indigo is a very special dye plant and—as is the case with woad, which can also be used to create blue—extracting its dye requires a certain amount of finesse. Fortunately, it is easy to buy powdered dyes that are already prepared and ready to use.

Unlike other dye powders, though, indigo powder is not hydrosoluble, which means it cannot be mixed with water except under certain conditions. The process required is what we call vat dyeing.

There are several kinds of indigo vats, but hydrosulfite, fructose, and iron are the most commonly used. I will be introducing you to an iron vat because it's ideal for beginners and is more environmentally friendly than a hydrosulfite vat (you can dump out the contents of an iron vat in your yard or compost). An iron indigo vat cannot be used with animal fibers because the presence of iron in the vat will damage the fibers.

The primary advantage of an indigo vat is that it is absolutely not necessary to mordant the fibers before dyeing them. You can also dye large quantities of fibers at one time: with 0.88 ounces (25 g) of powder you can dye between 1.1 pounds (500 grams) and 2.2 pounds (1 kilogram) of fiber, depending on the shade you want.

EQUIPMENT AND INGREDIENTS

- A non-reactive pot, cooking pot, basin, or bucket. I prefer the first option because it can be heated and reheated without having to transfer anything to another container and risk getting air into the dyebath.
- A wire basket or rack to be placed at the bottom of your vat (this is a must-have in the iron vat because a significant amount of sediment will be created at the bottom, and this could stain your fabric).
- Stainless steel tongs
- Scale
- A mason jar with four or five marbles to prepare the indigo mother.
- One part indigo (0.88 ounces [25 grams], for example), two parts ferrous sulfate (1.76 ounces [50 grams]), and three parts slaked lime (2.64 ounces [75 grams]). This ratio is why this vat is known as the 1, 2, 3 vat.

PREPARING THE VAT

STEP 1:

Fill your vat three-quarters of the way with water. Remove from heat when the water is not quite simmering yet. While your water is heating, prepare the mother. Pour the indigo powder into the jar. Add the marbles and a little water.

STEP 2:

Seal the jar and shake vigorously to form a paste.

STEP 3:

Pour some hot water from the vat (it should at least be steaming) into the mother jar and stir to combine.

STEP 4:

Add the ferrous sulfate and stir.

STEP 5:

Add the lime a little bit at a time, stirring between additions to avoid lumps. The liquid in the jar will change from blue to green to yellow. It will also start to develop a distinct odor.

STEP 6:

If the water in your vat has not heated up to just below a simmer, set aside your mother jar and wait. Once the water is at temperature, remove the vat from the heat and pour in the mother. Submerge the jar as you do this to prevent air from entering the vat. Let the marbles fall to the bottom of the vat and pick them out later.

STEP 7:

Stir carefully to prevent air from getting into the vat. A film should appear on the surface of your liquid.

STEP 8:

Insert the wire rack or basket in the bottom of the vat to protect your fabric from sediment deposits. Now your vat is ready.

DYEING

STEP 1:

Make sure your fabric is completely submerged when you add it to the vat. The bath should be a yellow-green color. Leave the fabric in the bath for 5 to 20 minutes depending on the color you are looking for.

STEP 2:

Your fabric should look green when you take it out of the vat. Oxidation will happen over time as it is exposed to air. Do your best to let as little air as possible into the vat each time you add or remove fibers. This means no vigorous stirring or splashing, no heavy dripping over the vat, etc.

STEP 3:

To facilitate oxidation, turn the fabric over and open any creases. When everything is blue, you can put the fabric back in the vat for 5 to 20 minutes. The dyeing process unfolds as you continue alternating between these immersions and oxidations.

STEP 4:

When oxidation is complete, wring out the fabric over a bowl or other container. Do not wring it out over the vat because this will let in air. The water you squeeze out can be added back to the vat for the next dye. Rinse your dyed fabrics in water and dry away from direct sunlight. The color will continue to oxidize.

STEP 5:

After a while, you will see that your vat has spoiled. The liquid will appear transparent, and your fabrics will no longer absorb any color. You can restart your vat by reheating the bath to just below boiling and adding some slaked lime to reduce it again. Stir gently and wait to see the signs of reduction you saw earlier (odor and film on the top). You can restart your vat this way several days or even several weeks later, if you're lucky. If you are trying to keep your vat going for longer periods of time, always store it at room temperature in a bucket with a lid.

Patterns and Printing

OMBRÉ DIP-DYEING

Dip-dyeing is an easy way to add variety to your dyed fabrics. There are several ways to do this.

First Method

Slowly dip your white fabric (premordanted and presoaked) into the dyebath one section at a time. Hanging the fabric above the pot using strings and clothespins (clipped to your stove hood or the edge of your pot, for example) will allow you to play around with different heights when dipping your fibers.

If you are hot dyeing, dip-dye the presoaked fabric in three 15-minute intervals. First, dip one-third of your fabric in the dyebath. This section will be the darkest. In the second stage, dip your piece of fabric halfway in for an in-between shade. To finish it off, dip the fabric three-quarters of the way in to create the palest section. If you are dyeing away from a heat source, heat your dyebath and transfer it to a clean receptacle. Dry the edges of the receptacle to avoid staining your fabric and submerge the fabric for several longer intervals (at least one hour for each section of fabric).

Second Method

If you want to play around with color pairings instead of darker and lighter shades of the same color, try this technique and dip a previously dyed piece of fabric in a second dyebath. Hibiscus looks lovely beside turmeric, and indigo blue works well with carrot top dye and the pink from almonds or madder.

Modifiers

You can also dip-dye using modifiers. Thanks to ferrous sulfate (iron), you can give your avocado pink fabric a purple-gray color and turn the warm tones of onion-dyed fibers into greens. Slaked lime can even turn your black bean blue fabric a lovely shade of aqua.

Creating your own unique dip-dye designs is easy if you choose to combine these techniques. You might decide, for example, to create your darkest section using a ferrous sulfate mixture and use a traditional dyebath for the in-between and paler sections of fabric.

This fabric was dyed with onion skins before being dipped in an almond dyebath.

An example of dip-dyeing with ferrous sulfate.

Tip

After submerging your previously dyed fabric in another dyebath, hang it to dry with your newest dye at the top. The fresh dye will stream down toward the bottom and create a gorgeous drip pattern.

CREATING DESIGNS WITH IRON WATER

Using iron water is a wonderful way to add patterns to plant-dyed fabrics. Dye your fabric and then paint, stamp, or try the shibori technique.

Painting

Work on a piece of dyed fabric that has been dried and ironed. Always make your line thinner than the result you want—the iron water will bleed into the fabric and thicken your line.

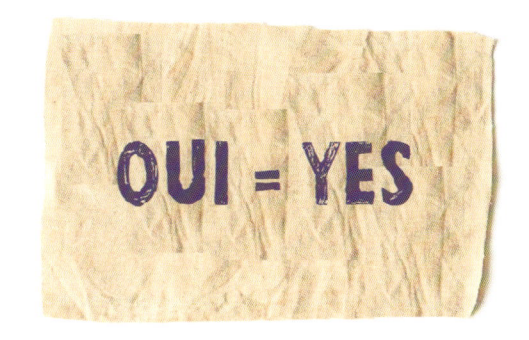

Stamping

Work on a piece of dyed fabric that has been dried and ironed. Moisten a piece of felt with the iron water. It should not be soaking wet. If it is too wet, just wring it out a little bit. Press your stamp down on the felt several times and then press down for three seconds on your dyed fabric. It tends to look a little smudgy until you really know how to do it, so do a few practice runs on small pieces of fabric to figure it out. Using stamps with simple, large designs helps, too.

Shibori

For this method, you can work with fabrics that are still damp. Once you have finished your folds, fill a bowl with water and add a small pinch of ferrous sulfate. Dip your fabric in the water for a few seconds to create your design (see page 108 for shibori techniques).

Splashing

Splashing can also be done on fabrics that are still damp. Do this outside or over a sink. Fill a bowl with iron water, dip your hand in, and fling drops of water onto the cloth with your fingers.

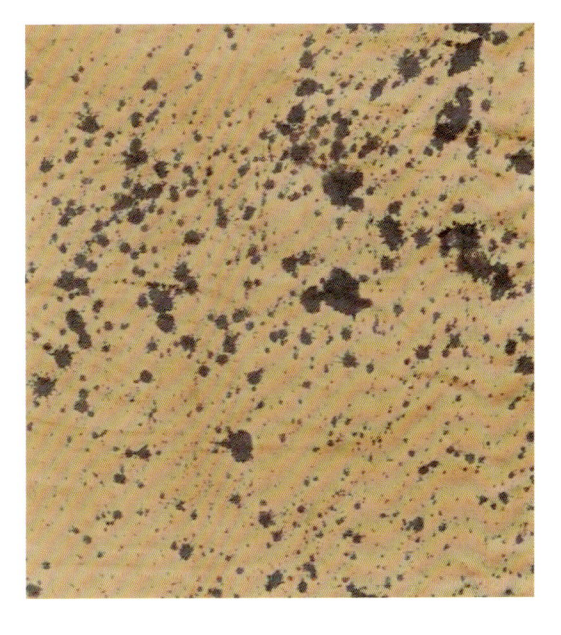

SHIBORI

This Japanese word refers to a range of folding and binding techniques that create patterns by preventing the dye from spreading. Indigo is the traditional dye used for shibori because—more than other dyes—it does not penetrate as easily into fabric folds. This makes it easier to restrict the dye to certain areas of the fabric. That being said, feel free to use other dyes for shibori projects as well. There are a variety of techniques that we will examine here.

Binding

Here are several binding techniques.

KANOKO SHIBORI

Tie knots around a twisted piece of fabric to create concentric circles. You can use rubber bands or twine.

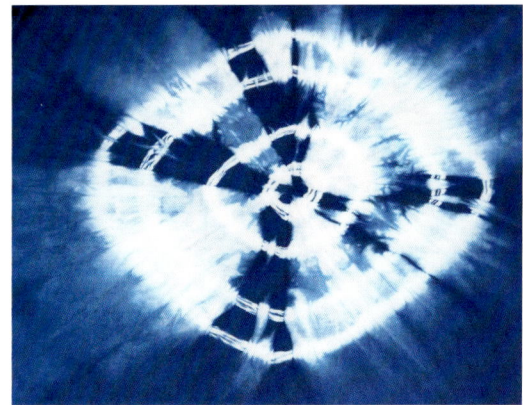

NE-MAKI SHIBORI

Wrap marbles or other small objects inside the fabric and tie them in place. This creates a pattern of small circles.

Clothespins and Clamps

ITAJIME SHIBORI

This technique involves sandwiching the folded fabric between two or more solid objects to hold it in place and create a pattern. You can use twine or rubber bands, but clamps are most effective. Recycled items like jar lids and bottle caps can be used to make circles. Wooden rods and the small wooden building blocks in the photos below also work well.

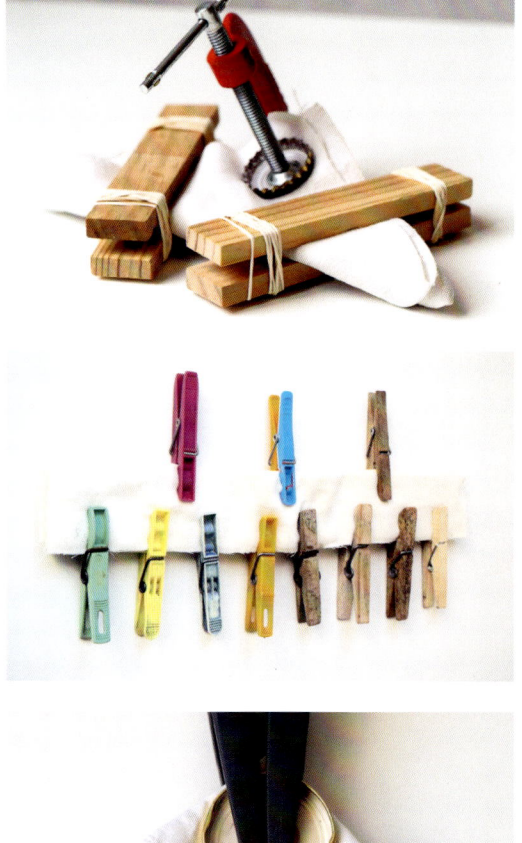

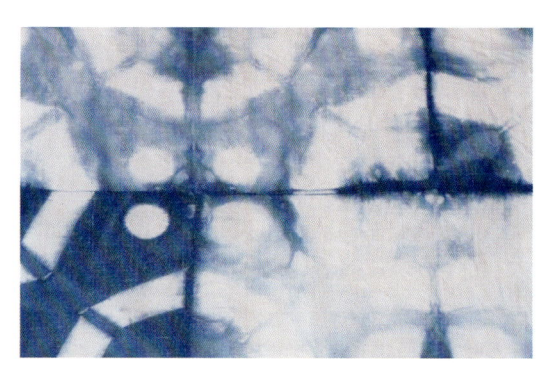

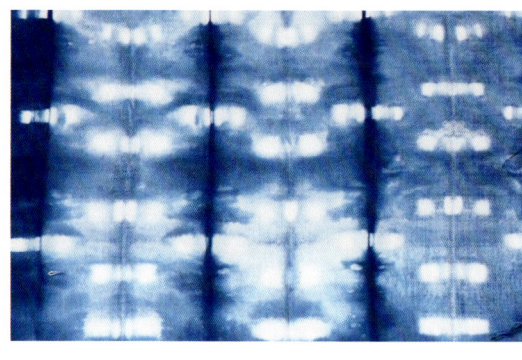

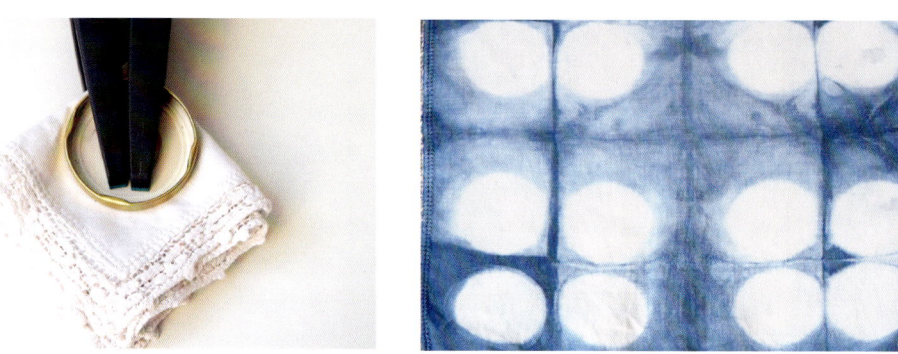

Folding

ARASHI SHIBORI

To create these thin stripes, fold your fabric in an accordion pattern and tie it in place before you dye. The fabric is typically tied around a cylindrical object. Here I used a bottle, but a piece of PVC pipe might be easier to dip.

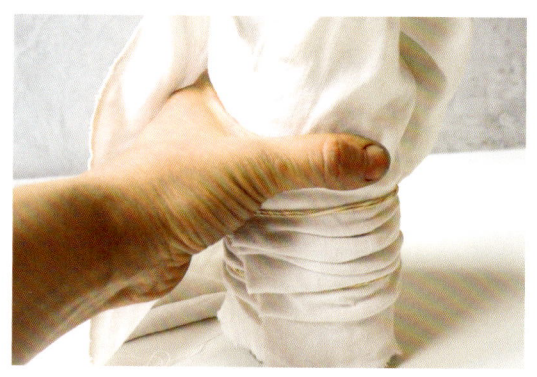

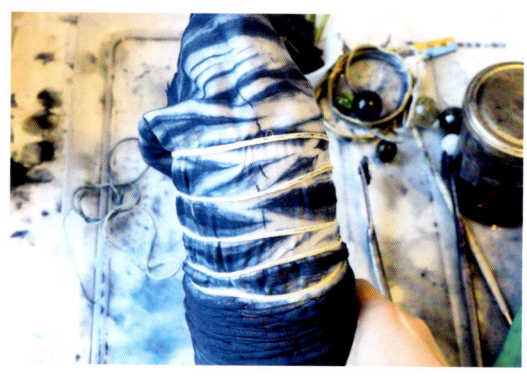
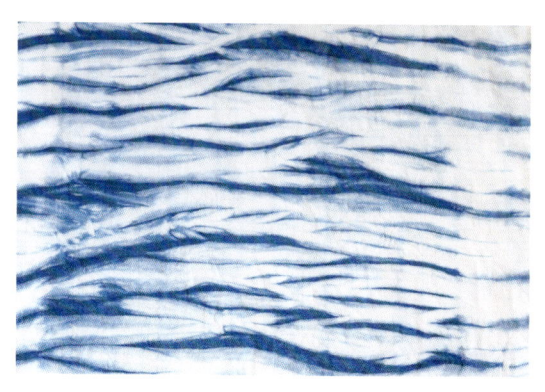

Sewing

NUI SHIBORI

First, stitch your pattern onto the fabric. Then pull the threads tight before submerging the fabric in your dyebath.

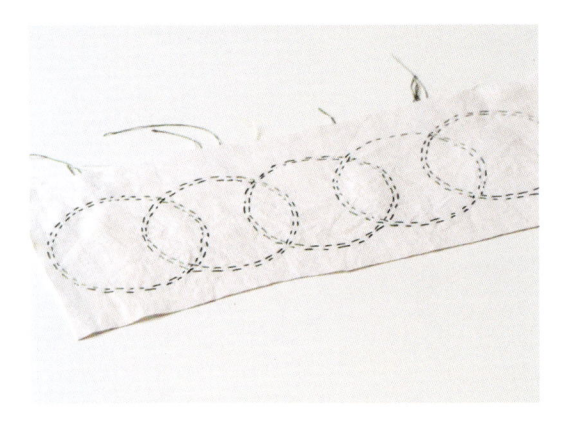

STEP 1:

Draw your pattern using erasable marker.

STEP 2:

Stitch over your drawing. Doubling each stitch will give you the best result. Use strong thread. Let 2 inches (5 cm) of thread hang off of the beginning and end of your stitching so you can pull tight at the end.

STEP 3:

Gather together all of the hanging threads and pull tight.

STEP 4:

Dye your fabric and let dry. Do not untie your stitches or unfold the fabric.

STEP 5:

Once the fabric is dry, undo your stitches and pull out the thread.

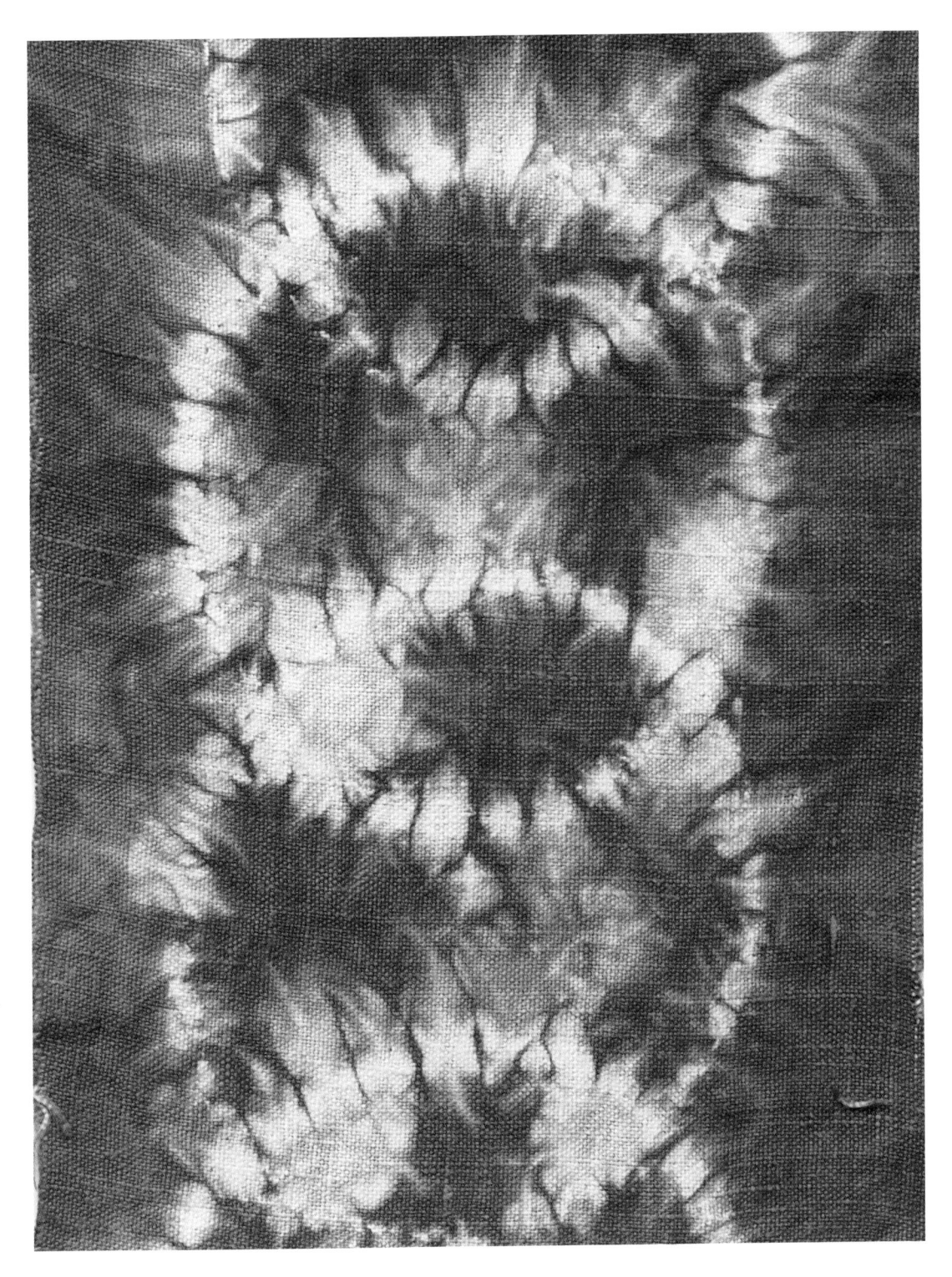

ICE DYEING

There is nothing traditional about this technique! Like eco-printing (page 120), it has recently grown in popularity thanks to dyers in North America and the United Kingdom. I've added a few variations of my own.

Ice dyeing is not difficult, and you are guaranteed to be pleasantly surprised once the process is over. The cold, just like the heat in hot dyeing, lets the fiber absorb the color more deeply.

The melting ice creates lighter and darker nuances of the same shade, and ice cubes of different colors that are placed next to each other will blend together to create a marbled, diluted effect.

Here are three different ways to do it.

First Method

Sprinkle dye powder over several ice cubes. This is the most common technique, but most of the plants that we're using (unlike chemical dyes) rarely come in powder form. You can certainly use those that do, though, like turmeric, madder, and cochineal. If you have large pieces of plant material, you can blend them up in a food processor and sprinkle that over the ice. It won't be as effective as a fine powder, but it will still give you results.

Second Method

Freeze your dyebaths! This is a method that I decided to test to fix the problem of powders mentioned above.

Once you have extracted the dye from your plants in the dyebath, let it cool. Next, fill an ice cube tray or other small plastic containers and put them in the freezer. This is a great way to recycle baths you've already used to dye something else. Once the ice has set, remove the cubes from the tray and keep them in a large container in your freezer. This way you can keep making dyebath cubes without having to look for other ice cube trays.

Third Method

Freeze your modifiers. If you freeze iron water or wood ash water into cubes and let them melt over tannin-dyed fabrics, you'll end up with an entrancing marbled effect (see December, page 154).

MATERIALS

- Wire cooling rack
- A tray or other container around 1 inch (a few centimeters) deep and the same diameter as the rack

STEP 1:

Place the rack over the tray. Wet your mordanted fabric and lay it on top of the rack. Scrunch up the fabric to form accordion pleats in every direction. Try not to let your folds get stuck on the underside of the fabric.

STEP 2:

Pile the ice cubes on top of the fabric. Use at least two different colors if you want marbling and blending.

STEP 3:

Let melt overnight or for a full day. The ice water will soak through the fabric and collect in the tray.

STEP 4:

Rinse thoroughly and dry away from sunlight.

ECO-PRINTING

This technique was invented by Australian dyer India Flint. It is different from traditional dyeing, but the results are just as beautiful and offer real surprises to those of us who are patient enough. Your finished eco-print may not always look the way you had imagined; sometimes the patterns will be dark and pronounced, sometimes they will appear as faint as ghosts! Keep in mind that there are a lot of factors at play: cooking time, how long you wait before opening the bundle, the plants you use, and the time of year you use them. The second half of spring is generally the best time because that is when a leaf's tannin content is peaking. Geranium leaves and plants from that family can be used all year round.

MATERIALS

- Flowers, leaves, onion skin scraps, etc.
- Sticks and white twine
- A steamer basket and pot to "cook" your bundles

Basic Eco-Printing

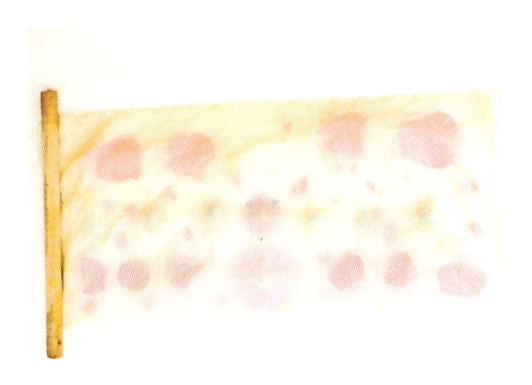

STEP 1:

Arrange your plant material on a piece of damp mordanted fabric. You can use flowers, small branches with berries, leaves, onion skin scraps, and/or hibiscus flowers. You can work on half of the fabric or the whole piece.

STEP 2:

Fold the fabric and roll it tightly around the stick.

STEP 3:

Tightly wrap the entire stick in white twine and tie in place.

STEP 4:

Steam the bundles for several hours (outdoors, if you can, because of the smell). If possible, leave them out in the sun for several days before unrolling them. Make several eco-prints at once instead of repeating this process over and over for one project at a time!

Eco-Printing with Iron

STEP 1:

Dry your plant material between two books or wooden planks to flatten it (this is optional).

STEP 2:

After a few days, rehydrate the leaves or flowers in an iron bath (one small glass of iron water for 2 quarts [roughly 2 liters] of water).

STEP 3:

Dry the leaves on a paper towel and then arrange them on top of your damp mordanted fabric.

STEP 4:

Follow the same steps you would for a basic eco-print, but this time roll up a piece of plastic or parchment paper with the fabric to hold in the iron water.

STEP 5:

After steaming for several hours, open your bundle and see if you are satisfied with the results. If not, you can dip the fabric in an iron bath to darken your print. Dry away from direct sunlight.

Variation

You can also "cook" your bundles in a dyebath and add a handful of ferrous sulfate (iron) to react with the tannins in your plants.

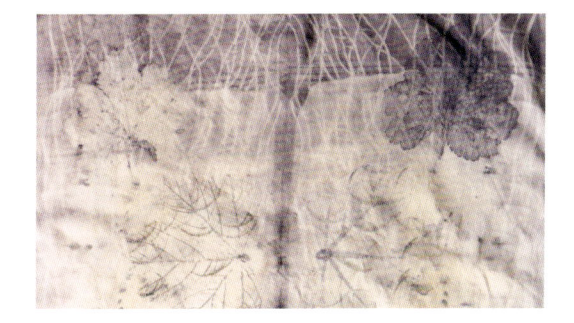

LEAF POUNDING

This is a very easy technique that's fun to do outside with children. The mallet liberates the tannins from the leaves and, thanks to iron water and oxidation, your prints will be indelible!

MATERIALS

- Tannic leaves
- White fabric
- A wooden board
- Masking tape
- Mallet (ideally made of plastic with a rounded head)
- Basin of iron water

You can try this with just about any leaf you can find outside, but know that if the print does not appear black in the bath, this means that the leaf is not tannic. The print will not stay green and will not hold up to washing.

STEP 1:
Place the leaf between two pieces of fabric.

STEP 2:
Use the mallet and pound firmly along the edges of the leaf. Avoid pounding too heavily in the center of the leaf or you will break it. You can turn the fabric over to see how the print looks, but don't worry if the green doesn't show through on the opposite side. Pounding should always be gentle, never too hard.

STEP 3:
Soak the fabric in a basin containing 2 quarts (roughly 2 liters) of water and ½ teaspoon ferrous sulfate (iron).

STEP 4:
After five minutes, rinse in soapy water followed by clean water. Dry in the open air to allow the tannins to oxidize.

DYEING YARN

Wool is one of the easiest materials to dye because it absorbs color easily and the results are always more intense than on cellulose fibers. And who can resist the fun of creating a one-of-a-kind ball of yarn for a future project?

For mordanting wool, take a look at page 16.

Ombré Dip-Dyeing

STEP 1:
Roll your yarn (premordanted, see page 16) into a tight ball and wet it.

STEP 2:
Submerge the ball in a dyebath. Try to find a small pot that is fairly tall (this is a fondue pot) and heat for 40 minutes, turning the yarn ball occasionally. Remove from heat and let rest overnight or until it has cooled completely.

STEP 3:
Rinse your yarn and squeeze out any dye liquid. When the water runs clear and the yarn is almost dry, wind and twist the yarn into a hank and leave to dry.

STEP 4:
Roll up the yarn so you can use it for knitting. Here is my result.

Stripes

STEP 1:
Wet a hank of yarn that has already been dyed (pictured here) or one that has been mordanted but not dyed (see step 1 of Speckles on page 128 for how to prepare the hank beforehand). As seen above, arrange the yarn in four glass jars containing two different dyebaths. Here I used oak gall + iron and madder on a hank that had already been dyed with dahlias.

STEP 2:
"Cook" your yarn in a water bath for 40 minutes. Let cool, rinse, and gently squeeze out any dye liquid.

Speckles

STEP 1:
Untwist the hank into a fairly large circle (use two chair backs around 3.25 feet [1 meter] apart).

STEP 2:
Tie small knots around sections of the untwisted hank to prevent tangling. Wet the yarn and place it on a tray or wire rack over a bowl or other container.

STEP 3:
Sprinkle plant material over the yarn. This could be a dye you purchase as a powder or a powder you prepare at home.

STEP 4:
If you use a salt or sugar shaker it will be easier to create the tiny flecks that make this technique so popular.

STEP 5:
Now wrap your untwisted hank of yarn in plastic (cellophane or a cut plastic bag that can be washed and reused). Make sure the different sections of your hank are not touching each other.

STEP 6:
Coil the wrapped tube into a spiral shape.

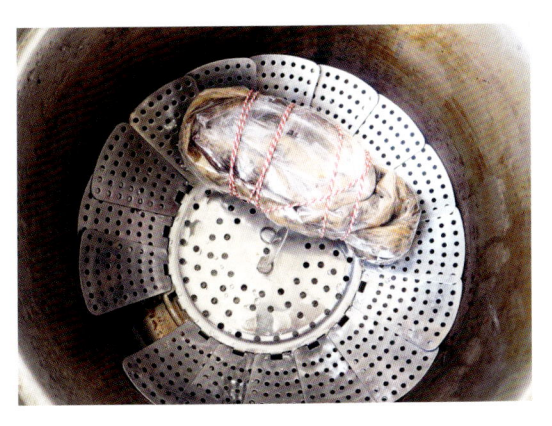 

STEP 7:
Tie it up and steam for 40 minutes. Let cool before rinsing.

STEP 8:
Let dry and twist your yarn back into a hank.

Projects

BORO CUSHION

Boro is an ancient traditional Japanese technique for patching clothing and household linens. Small pieces of fabric are layered on top of the damaged fabric and sewn together with parallel lines of running stitches. Here, I've given you a truly easy way to use up your dyed fabric scraps and create a customized pillowcase.

MATERIALS

- Monocolor pillowcase in natural fiber (linen in this case)
- Spun cotton thread of any color and a needle
- Dyed fabric scraps in various colors

STEP 1:

Pin the scraps onto the pillowcase to "sketch out" your mosaic.

STEP 2:

Use two strands of thread and a fairly long needle to sew lines of running stitches. Make sure to space them evenly and try to stagger the rows.

SAVING A STAINED GARMENT

People often think that you can give a stained piece of clothing new life with a little bit of dye, but unfortunately this is nearly impossible. The stain will just reappear after the dyeing process! To find a solution to this problem, sometimes I cheat and drown out the original stain under other "stains" I make with iron water.

MATERIALS

- Stained garment made from natural fibers (mordant before dyeing for best results)
- Plastic bag and rubber band (if you want to dip-dye)
- Bowl and iron water
- Birch bark dyebath (page 77) or other tannic dye

STEP 1:

Seal the bottom of the garment inside the plastic bag and secure it with the rubber band. The stained area should be outside the bag.

STEP 2:

Heat the bath and submerge only the stained section of the garment. Remove after around 45 minutes and soak the garment in a basin of water.

The dye will bleed and the undipped section of garment outside the bag will absorb some color, creating an ombré effect.

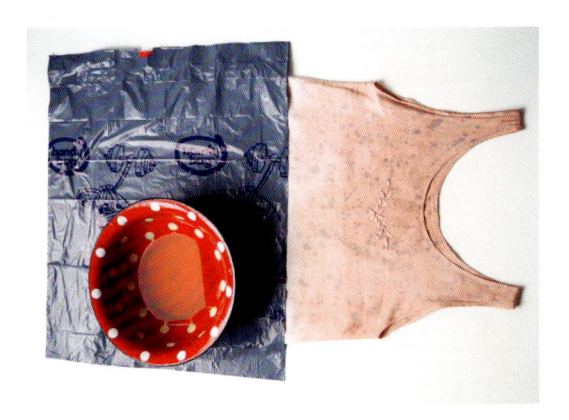

STEP 3:

Lay the garment flat on a board or table and cover the undyed area with a plastic bag.

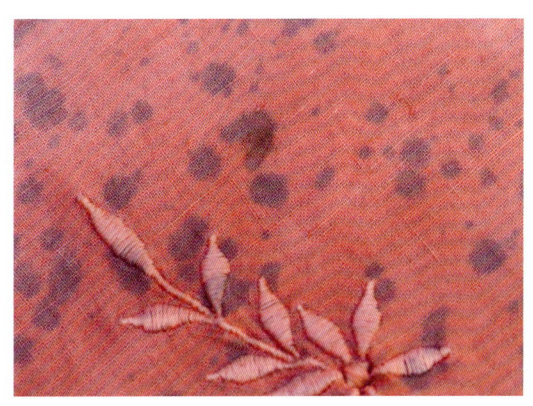

STEP 4:

Pour the iron water into a bowl and use your hands to splash the garment. As you work, make sure you splash the stained area, too.

DISH TOWEL TRIO WITH KITCHEN SCRAPS

I'm sure you have dish towels in your kitchen that could use a little freshening up for spring. I'll show you how to use kitchen waste to give them a new look.

MATERIALS

- White dish towels made of cotton or linen
- Avocado skins, black bean soaking water, and an old bouquet of daffodils

STEP 1:

If necessary, revive and brighten your white towels by boiling them in water with sodium percarbonate and Marseille soap (or see page 25 for a Castile soap detergent formula). Mordant with alum. Your dish towels will have to endure frequent washing at high temperatures and if you skip mordanting, the color simply will not last. Follow the steps for dyeing with avocados and black bean water on pages 81 and 91.

STEP 2:

Cut up your daffodil bouquet—flowers, stems, and all. Into your dye pot, pour the water from the vase and then add more water along with your flowers and stems. Heat for one hour. Halfway through, blend with an immersion blender.

STEP 3:

Strain the liquid and submerge your dish towel in the dyebath. Heat for 45 minutes or less. You can dip the towel in wood ash water to make the color even richer.

SILK SHIRT ECO-PRINT

April

Take advantage of the tannin-rich young plants that emerge every spring to completely transform an old silk top. This can be done on other natural fibers, too, but the results on silk are more attractive.

MATERIALS

- Silk top (mordant ahead of time if desired)
- Tannic tree and shrub leaves (oak, chestnut, fern, strawberry, raspberry) and other plant material in small pieces or powder form. I used hibiscus flowers and madder root.
- Stick, twine, and a pot with a steamer basket

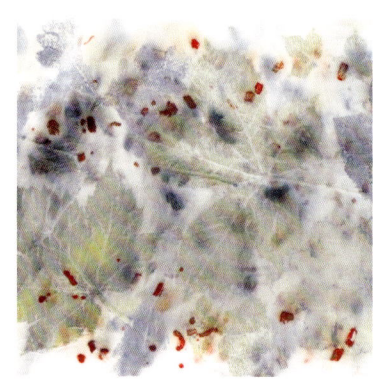

STEP 1:

Arrange your plant material on the upper half of the garment and sprinkle with tiny pieces of dried hibiscus flowers and madder root (or other plant powders).

STEP 2:

Fold the garment and roll it up around a stick. Secure with twine.

STEP 3:

Steam for two or three hours. Untie the twine and remove the plant material.

STEP 4:

Submerge the garment in an iron bath to deepen the color of your printed pattern. The neon yellow of certain plants will darken and turn green. Dyes like madder and hibiscus will also change after contact with iron. Rinse in soapy water and dry away from sunlight. The oxidation process will continue.

BOTANICAL MURAL

Springtime is in full swing by now and all of the plants are out! Preserve this special time of year with a wall of pounded leaf prints using leaves from your yard or region. What could be better?

MATERIALS

- Embroidery hoops in different sizes
- Mallet
- White cotton fabric (no need for mordanting)
- Plants, tannic if possible
- Basin of iron water
- Erasable fabric marker, embroidery thread, and a needle

Return to page 124 for a detailed explanation of the leaf pounding technique.

STEP 1:

Place the fabric in your hoop and embroider the name of the plant (optional).

STEP 2:

Glue the excess fabric to the wood on the back of the hoop.

"MERCI" TOTE

Here's a quick and inexpensive way to make an end-of-year gift for a teacher. The oak gall used here allows you to dye the bag without mordanting beforehand and yields a rich, dark color that will make the letters pop.

MATERIALS

- Organic cotton tote bag
- Natural wooden letters (you will need two of each letter)
- 10 small wooden blocks and rubber bands
- Oak gall dyebath (page 93)

STEP 1:

Decide how you want to arrange the letters and then set them aside.

Fold the bag into quarters in an accordion pattern. Keep the band of fabric where you will place your letters facing you. Pay attention to which direction the letters need to be pointing.

STEP 2:

Take your two Ms and place one on each side of the fold so they are sandwiching the bag between them. Now secure them in place with two wooden blocks and rubber bands. Wrap the rubber bands as tightly as you can (use two for increased resistance). Repeat this process until you have finished the word.

Soak the whole bag and add to the dyebath.

Heat for 10 to 15 minutes. Rinse and remove the wooden blocks and letters.

MESH SHOPPING BAGS

Mesh bags are back in style and organic white cotton ones can usually be found in health food stores or online. They are also easy to dye and will absorb color well because they are lightweight and are made using only small amounts of fabric.

MATERIALS

- White mesh bags
- Black bean dyebath (page 91)
- Pomegranate dyebath (page 49)

STEP 1:
Mordant the bags (see page 16).

STEP 2:
Submerge in the dyebaths. Heat for one hour. The blue net bag was left in a glass jar overnight because I had used the dyebath for another project already and I wanted to exhaust it.

STEP 3:
For the dip-dyed bag, I used a knitting needle to hang the bag so that only half of the bag was in the liquid.

The little yellow bag was dipped in wood ash after dyeing, which is why it's a deeper bronze color.

INDIGO PAREO

Dip a simple white cotton tablecloth in an indigo vat and you'll instantly have the perfect pareo (sometimes called a sarong) to bring to the beach or a country picnic.

MATERIALS

- White cotton tablecloth
- 3 clamps
- 18 small wooden blocks
- Indigo vat (page 95)

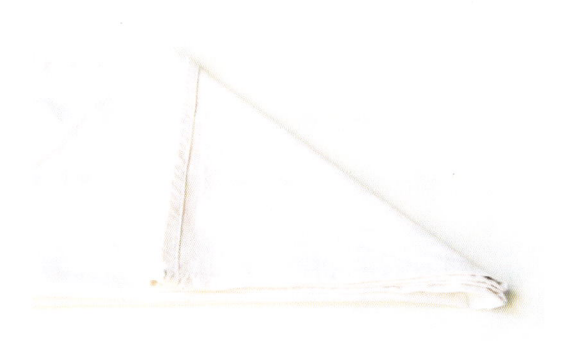

STEP 1:
Fold the tablecloth lengthwise in an accordion pattern and then make a right triangle by folding down one end.

STEP 2:
Continue folding this way—turning the whole piece over and over—until the whole tablecloth has been folded into a triangle. If there's a small piece left at the end, just fold it under.

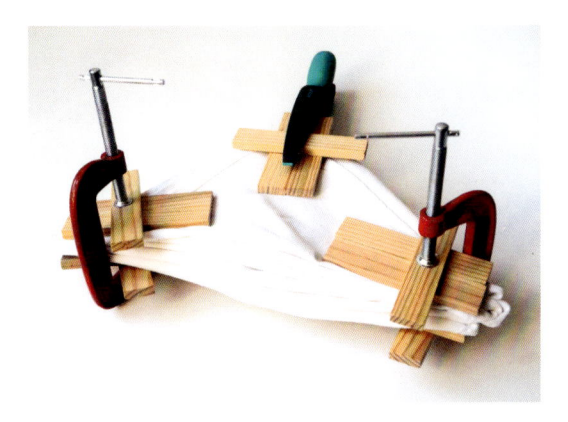

STEP 3:
Attach the wooden blocks to each corner as seen in the photo.

STEP 4:
Now make sure everything will fit in your indigo vat. Follow the instructions for dyeing with an iron indigo vat (page 95).

PRINTED LEAF T-SHIRT

September

It's time to use up the last of the oak leaves before autumn arrives and scatters them to the ground. Customizing a T-shirt is a great place to start. Oak leaves are the easiest leaves to work with because of their high tannin content and their simple shape, but you can use others if you prefer.

MATERIALS

- Garment made of natural fibers (linen jersey is what I used)
- One mallet, two small wooden boards, and masking tape
- Oak leaves
- A basin of water and a pinch of ferrous sulfate (iron)

STEP 1:
Arrange the leaves around the neckline of the shirt.

STEP 2:
Secure the leaves with masking tape. Insert a wooden board between the front and back of the shirt to avoid staining it. Now you can follow the instructions for leaf pounding.

STEP 3:
Remove the tape.

STEP 4:
Prepare an iron water bath. Only use a small amount of ferrous sulfate (iron) because otherwise it will turn your white garment a pale yellow-gray.

STEP 5:
Soak the shirt for a few minutes. Remove from the bath and dry away from sunlight to allow oxidation to take place.

DYED DOILY PLANT HANGERS

There are usually piles of antique doilies in thrift stores and this project is a way to give them a more contemporary look. These hangers are made from crocheted cotton, so they are easy to dye. They will also save you floor space when it's time to bring plants inside for the winter.

MATERIALS

- Antique white doilies, round or rectangular
- White rope, around 16.4 feet (5 meters) per doily
- 4 clothespins and a knitting needle or long wooden rod
- String
- Avocado dyebath (page 81)
- Iron bath (optional, page 31)

STEP 1:
Using the clothespins, string, and wooden rod, build a hanging rack over your pot where you can pin your doilies so they are only partially submerged.

STEP 2:
Heat the pot for 45 minutes minimum.

STEP 3:
(Optional) When your dyebath is finished, wring out the doily without rinsing it and dip the edge in an iron bath for two or three minutes. Dry and allow to oxidize.

STEP 4:
When the doilies are dry, lay them flat. Cut eight pieces of rope that are all about the same length. Tie one length of rope to each of eight evenly spaced points on the doily's edge. Now you can tie them all together in one large knot at the top or tie the tip of each rope to the rope next to it to create a macrame pattern.

ALL-NATURAL WOODEN STROLLER CHAIN

November

If you already use small wooden rods for your shibori projects, you've probably realized that plant dyes really leave their mark on wood. Like cotton and linen, wood is made of cellulose. If it is unfinished, it will readily absorb color from the dye.

MATERIALS

- Unfinished wooden beads
- 2 suspender clips
- 1 piece of cotton rope
- Oak gall + iron dyebath (pages 93 and 31)
- Pomegranate dyebath (page 49)
- Oak dyebath (page 67)
- Birch dyebath (page 77)
- Eucalyptus dyebath (page 63)

STEP 1:

Pour your dyebaths into five glass jars. Add your beads to the jars and heat in a water bath for fifteen minutes before sealing the jar. If you have extra pieces of bark, leave them in the jar with the beads.

STEP 2:

Let the beads steep for two days. Shake the jars now and then.

STEP 3:

Remove the beads from the dyebaths and dry.

STEP 4:

When the beads are dry, thread them onto the rope and make your stroller chain.

STEP 5:

Attach your suspender clips to the ends of the rope. These will allow you to clip the beads onto a stroller, bag, or highchair. Make sure your knots are tight so the beads can't slip off.

FUROSHIKI GIFT WRAP

Furoshiki are beautiful squares of fabric that can be used to wrap presents and then be reused again and again. Why not make your own to share at Christmas? Here I've used a variation on the ice dyeing technique explained on page 117. These ice cubes will be made with iron water.

MATERIALS

- White cotton handkerchiefs
- Iron water ice cubes (page 31)
- Wire rack and tray
- Pomegranate dyebath (page 49)

Even though you will only be using one dyebath, your fabric squares will be two-toned. You can use a variety of different tannic plants, but pomegranate will give you the best result for your efforts because it is such a powerful dye. All of the squares pictured here were dyed with the peel of a single pomegranate! I dyed in one bath first and got the darker squares, and then I dyed again in a second dyebath that was paler in color.

STEP 1:

Get your hands on some old white handkerchiefs and give them a wash. Mordanting is not required. Between the ice dyeing and the iron water, any small stains on your handkerchiefs will be easily hidden. Follow the instructions for pomegranate peel as explained on page 49. Pour the iron water into your ice cube tray and leave it to set in the freezer.

STEP 2:

Wet your handkerchiefs and lay them on the wire rack over the tray. Scrunch up the fabric and pile three or four large ice cubes on each square (if you would like the colors to be stronger, you can repeat the process). Wait until the cubes melt completely before rinsing and drying.

Resources

North American Online Stores

Dharma Trading Co. / dharmatrading.com: This company offers a wide range of products for natural dyeing, including vegetable dyes, mordants, natural fibers, and specialized tools.

Botanical Colors / botanicalcolors.com: This store specializes in natural dyes and offers plant extracts, dye kits, ecological mordants, and online workshops to learn plant dyeing techniques.

Maiwa / maiwa.com: Although based in Canada, Maiwa is very popular in the United States. It offers a variety of natural dyes, fibers, fabrics, and tools, as well as educational resources on vegetable dyeing.

Aurora Silk / aurorasilk.com: This store offers natural dyes, fibers, and fabrics, with a focus on sustainable and eco-friendly practices.

Earthues / earthues.com: Specializing in natural dyes, Earthues offers plant extracts, mordants, and workshops for dyers of all levels.

British Online Stores

Wild Colours / www.wildcolours.co.uk: Specializing in vegetable dyes, Wild Colors offers a wide range of natural extracts, dye plants such as madder and indigo, as well as accessories for dyeing.

George Weil & Sons / www.georgeweil.com: George Weil is a recognized supplier to textile artists that offers natural dyes, fibers, yarns, fabrics, and dyeing tools.

Myrobalan / www.myrobalan.co.uk: Specializing in ecological vegetable dyes, Myrobalan offers natural extracts, dye plants, and environmentally friendly mordants. They maintain a sustainable and ethical approach.

Fiery Felts / www.fieryfelts.co.uk: A store specializing in textile arts that offers natural dye kits, fabrics, fibers, and products for craft creation, as well as materials for felting and creative dyeing.

Books

The Modern Natural Dyer: A Comprehensive Guide to Dyeing Silk, Wool, Linen, and Cotton at Home
Author: Kristine Vejar
This book offers a comprehensive approach to natural dyeing at home, covering fibers such as silk, wool, linen, and cotton. It provides detailed instructions and practical projects for each fiber type.

Wild Color: The Complete Guide to Making and Using Natural Dyes
Author: Jenny Dean
This exhaustive guide explores the use of natural dyes, with instructions on fiber preparation, color extraction, and dye application. It also includes a directory of dye plants.

Botanical Colour at Your Fingertips
Author: Rebecca Desnos
This book focuses on plant-based dyeing without the use of metallic mordants, highlighting gentle, environmentally friendly methods for dyeing textiles.

Journeys in Natural Dyeing: Techniques for Creating Color at Home
Author: Kristine Vejar and Adrienne Rodriguez
The authors share natural dyeing techniques inspired by their travels, offering a global perspective on dyeing practices and projects to try at home.

Natural Dyeing: Learn How to Create Colour and Dye Textiles Naturally
Author: Kathryn Davey
This book covers the entire natural dyeing process, from fiber preparation to color extraction, with simple instructions and practical projects.

Websites Highlighting Natural Dyers

Botanical Colors
This site offers a range of natural dyes, tutorials, and resources for dyers. It highlights artists and natural dyers through interviews and case studies.
Website: www.botanicalcolors.com

The Modern Natural Dyer
Run by Kristine Vejar, author and dyer, this site complements her book and provides tutorials, online workshops, and resources on natural dyeing, featuring projects and collaborations with other dyers.
Website: www.moderndyer.com

Rebecca Desnos

A dyer and author, Rebecca shares blog articles, tutorials, and e-books on plant-based dyeing, focusing on eco-friendly methods and showcasing work from other artists in the field.

Website: www.rebeccadesnos.com

Instagram Accounts Highlighting Natural Dyers

A Verb for Keeping Warm

This account showcases naturally dyed textile creations, workshops, and resources on natural dyeing.

Instagram: www.instagram.com/averbforkeepingwarm

Natural Dyer

Managed by a passionate dyer, this account features insights into natural dye projects, tips, and tutorials.

Instagram: www.instagram.com/naturaldyer

The Dogwood Dyer

This account highlights eco-dyeing techniques, workshops, and collaborations with other artists.

Instagram: www.instagram.com/thedogwooddyer

Sustainably Dyed

Focused on sustainable dyeing, this account shares natural dyeing processes, inspirations, and eco-friendly tips.

Instagram: www.instagram.com/sustainablydyed

Plant Dyed Goods

This account showcases plant-dyed items, tutorials, and information about the dye plants used.

Instagram: www.instagram.com/plantdyedgoods

TikTok accounts dedicated to natural dyeing, where creators share their techniques, tips, and inspirations:

Tasmiyas Creations
Description: Discover the art of handmade natural dyeing techniques for textiles like wool, silk, and cotton. Explore the use of natural dyes such as indigo, madder, and turmeric to create beautiful, eco-friendly fabrics.
TikTok: www.tiktok.com/@crafty.needles

Jamie Young
Description: Unleash your creativity with natural dyeing techniques using plants and flowers. Learn about eco-printing and hapa-zome to incorporate nature's beauty into your fabric creations.
TikTok: www.tiktok.com/@thebarefootdyer

Real Rural Life
Description: Explore the art of dyeing cloth with natural materials and vibrant colors. Learn about the process of creating unique, eco-friendly clothing.
TikTok: www.tiktok.com/@realrural_life

DesignLabGive
Description: Discover natural dyeing projects using avocado skins and pits, along with other natural materials. Get a behind-the-scenes look at workshops and creative processes.
TikTok: www.tiktok.com/@designlabgive

Nettles and Petals
Description: Learn how to use vibrant coreopsis flowers for natural dyeing and printmaking in your garden. Enhance your crafting with versatile and beneficial flowers.
TikTok: www.tiktok.com/@nettlesandpetals

ACKNOWLEDGMENTS

A huge thank you to my husband for putting up with me while I transformed into a witch for a few months. He endured my many pots, the suspicious odors in the kitchen, and strange jars left in every corner of our house.

Thank you to my lovely models, Anouk, Oscar, and Gabriel, and to the people who allowed me to borrow their beautiful gardens: Longuetoise, Audrey and Thomas. Thank you to Gaëlle for her flowers and her beautiful letters. Thank you to Pauline and my mother for lending their knitting talents. I would also like to thank Linda Louis for her valuable advice and magnificent photos.

And lastly, thank you to the team at Mango who placed their trust in me once again for a second book.

Copyright © 2025 by Camille Binet-Dezert
First published in August 2018 as *Teintures et impressions végétales* by Éditions Mango.

Skyhorse Publishing books may be purchased in bulk at special discounts for sales promotion, corporate gifts, fund-raising, or educational purposes. Special editions can also be created to specifications. For details, contact the Special Sales Department, Skyhorse Publishing, 307 West 36th Street, 11th Floor, New York, NY 10018 or info@skyhorsepublishing.com.

Skyhorse® and Skyhorse Publishing® are registered trademarks of Skyhorse Publishing, Inc.®, a Delaware corporation.

Visit our website at www.skyhorsepublishing.com.

10 9 8 7 6 5 4 3 2 1

Library of Congress Cataloging-in-Publication Data is available on file.

Layout: Élise Bonhomme
Photography: Linda Louis, except for the cover: Fabrice Besse (styling, Sonia Roy)

Print ISBN: 978-1-5107-8301-0
Ebook ISBN: 978-1-5107-8390-4

Printed in China